EVENTS & OUTCOMES
THE
FRENCH REVOLUTION

STEWART ROSS

RAINTREE STECK-VAUGHN PUBLISHERS

A Harcourt Company

Austin   New York
www.raintreesteckvaughn.com

Library of Congress Cataloging-in-Publication Data
is available upon request

ISBN 0-7398-5798-3

Printed in Spain. Bound in the United States.

1 2 3 4 5 6 7 8 9 0 LB 06 05 04 03 02

Edited by Rachel Norridge
Designed by Neil Sayer
Consultant: Dr Tony McCulloch

Acknowledgments

Cover image: The Bridgeman Art Library **p. 4** The Bridgeman Art Library **p. 6** Mary Evans Picture Library **p. 7** Mary Evans Picture Library **p. 8** Mary Evans Picture Library **p. 9** Mary Evans Picture Library **p. 10** Roger-Viollet **p. 11** the art archive **p. 12** the art archive **p. 13** the art archive **p. 14** Mary Evans Picture Library **p. 15** The Bridgeman Art Library **p. 16** Mary Evans Picture Library **p. 17** (top) The Bridgeman Art Library, (bottom) Mary Evans Picture Library **p. 18** Mary Evans Picture Library **p. 19** (top) Mary Evans Picture Library, (bottom) The Bridgeman Art Library **p. 20** Mary Evans Picture Library **p. 21** (top) The Bridgeman Art Library, (bottom) the art archive **p. 22** Mary Evans Picture Library **p. 23** (top) Mary Evans Picture Library, (bottom) The Bridgeman Art Library **p. 24** (top) Mary Evans Picture Library, (bottom) Roger-Viollet **p. 25** (top) Roger-Viollet, (bottom) the art archive **p. 26** The Bridgeman Art Library **p. 27** The Bridgeman Art Library **p. 28** Mary Evans Picture Library **p. 29** The Bridgeman Art Library **p. 30** the art archive **p. 31** Mary Evans Picture Library **p. 32** The Bridgeman Art Library **p. 33** (top) Mary Evans Picture Library, (bottom) the art archive **p. 34** Mary Evans Picture Library **p. 35** Roger-Viollet **p. 36** the art archive **p. 37** (top) the art archive, (bottom) Mary Evans Picture Library **p. 38** the art archive **p. 39** the art archive **p. 40** The Bridgeman Art Library **p. 41** Mary Evans Picture Library **p. 42** Roger-Viollet **p. 43** The Bridgeman Art Library **p. 44** Mary Evans Picture Library **p. 45** The Bridgeman Art Library **p. 46** the art archive **p. 47** Roger-Viollet **p. 48** the art archive **p. 49** Mary Evans Picture Library **p. 50** the art archive **p. 51** (top) the art archive, (bottom) Mary Evans Picture Library **p. 52** (top) the art archive, (bottom) Mary Evans Picture Library **p. 53** Mary Evans Picture Library **p. 54** The Bridgeman Art Library **p. 55** the art archive **p. 56** (top) the art archive, (bottom) Mary Evans Picture Library **p. 57** the art archive **p. 58** Mary Evans Picture Library **p. 59** The Bridgeman Art Library **p. 60** The Bridgeman Art Library **p. 61** (top) Mary Evans Picture Library, (bottom) The Bridgeman Art Library **p. 62** (top) Mary Evans Picture Library, (bottom) Roger-Viollet **p. 63** Roger-Viollet **p. 64** Mary Evans Picture Library **p. 65** Roger-Viollet **p. 66** The Bridgeman Art Library **p. 67** (top) Mary Evans Picture Library, (bottom) Roger-Viollet **p. 69** The Bridgeman Art Library **p. 70** Topham Picturepoint **p. 71** (top) Topham Picturepoint, (bottom) The Bridgeman Art Library **p. 72** Topham Picturepoint

CONTENTS

THE GREAT UPHEAVAL

Three Revolutions

Three great revolutions ushered in the modern era. The first was England's Glorious and Bloodless Revolution of 1688–1689, which gave political form to the principles of constitutional monarchy and representative government. The second, introducing self-determination, republicanism, and the written constitution, was the American Revolution of 1775–1783. The third, and the most dramatic, was the French Revolution of 1789–1795.

What was this revolution about? In the simplest terms, it was a series of events that overturned France's traditional social and political structure (based on an hereditary monarchy, privilege, and the Roman Catholic Church) and replaced it with a new structure based—at least in theory—on human rights, liberty, equality, and fraternity.

Signing the American Declaration of Independence, 1776. The Declaration's principles were widely praised in France, America's ally in the struggle with Great Britain.

Constitutional monarchy, 1689: The English crown is offered to Princess Mary and her Dutch husband, William of Orange.

Even from a rather simple summary, it is clear that the revolution in France was different in scope from its English and American predecessors. The peaceful English Revolution did not so much bring about changes as confirm those that had been taking place for at least half a century. The American Revolution marked a significant break with the past but generally left the pre-revolutionary political and social elite intact. Neither matches the French Revolution for the speed and scope of its impact.

Questions and Answers

An event so momentous as the French Revolution inevitably raises a huge number of questions about its causes, nature, and effect. Historians have struggled to reach agreement on answers to many of them. There is little agreement on seemingly simple questions, such as when the Revolution started and finished. Few topics in history have been as hotly debated as the Revolution's causes. More recently, the traditional focus on events in Paris has been adjusted by the hundreds of local studies that reveal the Revolution to have been a far more complex and diverse (and therefore less easily summarized) phenomenon than previously thought.

Nevertheless, historians are all agreed on one thing: The French Revolution was enormously important. This was recognized at the time when news of its most famous event, the fall of the Bastille, sent shivers of delight or horror (depending on whether the recipient was for or against the monarchy and noble classes) across the Western world and beyond. Not surprisingly, it is still widely celebrated in France to this day.

Behind the Image

The events in France captured the popular imagination in a manner that has been matched by no other revolution. The images they brought forth, as much Hollywood as history, remain as powerful today as when they occurred: the swirling, shrieking mob; an isolated, pleasure-loving `queen; the deadly swish of the guillotine; elated soldiers marching to the *Marseillaise*; and the pale revolutionary leader bleeding to death in his bath. As memorable as such images are, they were only the visible signs of profound changes. The French Revolution altered France forever and had a startling impact elsewhere for years to come.

Monarchy on the brink: The Parisian mob mocks Louis XVI after breaking into the Tuileries Palace in 1792.

Citizens Instead of Subjects

In the French Revolution, ideas that had been tossed around for decades were suddenly given practical form. Government took on a new meaning: It was no longer the special arena of the privileged, exercised as a fatherly, even God-given duty. Instead, it was a trust from the people, from whom it gained its authority. Its purpose was no longer the preservation of law and order and the status quo; it existed to benefit the people it served, to protect their rights and promote their happiness.

Citizens replaced subjects (a linguistic change not recognized by monarchies like Britain for almost two centuries), and the law was there to protect them all, whatever their position in society. The last relics of the medieval system known as feudalism were swept away. No man (woman's turn was to come later) was now born better or worse than anyone else. This principle alone distinguishes the French from the American Revolution. Although there seemed to be a feverish struggle for human rights, America remained a slave-owning nation for more than 70 years after the start of its revolution.

Fighting for freedom. Inspired by the Revolution's call for liberty, the French government abolished slavery in the colonies in 1794. Although Napoleon reversed this decision, the people of Saint-Domingue (shown here fighting off French troops) successfully established the independent republic of Haiti in 1802.

Nationalism

Beyond France's borders, the Revolution brought hope to millions. It showed what ordinary people, united and inspired, could achieve by their own efforts. From this grew a force that dominated international affairs in the 19th and 20th centuries: nationalism.

Nationalism was nothing new in the late 18th century. What was new was the tribal intensity the Revolution produced in the French and other peoples. It became a force for change, breaking up old empires and creating new countries. It inspired magnificent heroism and supreme achievements in the arts and science. However, it also bred outrageous intolerance and cruelty. It was the nuclear power of the early modern world, bearing benefits and horrors in equal measure.

Revolution or Peaceful Changes

The same may be said of the Revolution as a whole. What began as an inspiring triumph of the human spirit ended in war, bloodshed, dictatorship, and finally, a partial restoration of the old order. It made violence a virtue, trampled on the rights of minorities, and showed how a dedicated band of well-organized extremists could exploit the hopes and fears of the people to its own ends—a tactic learned by future generations of would-be tyrants of both the extreme left and right.

The French Revolution became a counterexample to the political model favored by the western world. While the latter offered peaceful changes, the French instead offered the more romantic quick-fix of drastic revolution. However, violence, once begun, was not easily ended—which is the main reason why the French Revolution remains as controversial today as it always has been.

The legacy of violence: The power of the mob became a force for change.

TO THE BASTILLE

CHAPTER ONE

The *Ancien Régime*

The France that collapsed in revolution in 1789 is known as the "*Ancien [old] Régime*." It was not an organized system of government and society, but had developed bit by bit over many centuries. As a result, it was full of inequalities and contradictions. This produced tensions that, when the government failed to defuse them, boiled over into revolution.

France was made up of a wide variety of provinces, regions, towns and cities, corporations, guilds, and other organizations, all of which clung proudly to their rights. The largest and richest corporation was the Church.

An 18th-century map showing the regions of France. The country was a collection of royal territories gathered together by successive monarchs, rather than a nation state.

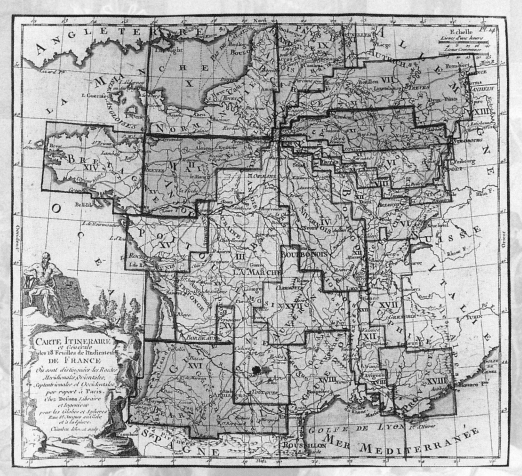

The Monarchy

Although the French king is commonly referred to as "absolute," his powers were far from tyrannical—for example, the Church owed ultimate allegiance to the Pope. Nevertheless, the king was the focus of the state, and policy depended on his initiatives. Louis XIV (1643–1715) had ruled with great skill. Louis XV (1715–1774) maintained his great-grandfather's system but made little effort to adapt it to changing circumstances. Indeed, with surprising foresight he declared,

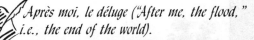 *Après moi, le déluge ("After me, the flood," i.e., the end of the world).*

His successor, Louis XVI (1774–1792), lacked the intelligence and political skills of his two predecessors. By the time of his reign, the cracks in the *Ancien Régime* had widened into gaping holes, and the outlook for the monarchy was not promising.

The Sun King: Louis XIV, king of 20 million subjects, presided over the richest and most sophisticated court in Europe.

Parlements

The existence of so many groups claiming legal privileges (which we would call "rights") led to frequent clashes of interest. This played into the hands of one of the richest and most influential groups in French society, the lawyers. Royal edicts, for instance, did not have the force of law until they were registered by regional assemblies of noble lawyers, known as *parlements*. The lawyers were generally conservative because they made a living from interpreting existing privileges. Under such circumstances, change was almost impossible.

The Three Estates

French society was divided into three groups, or "estates." The first was the clergy and the second the hereditary nobility; both were small in number (about 500,000 out of around 26 million), but deeply privileged. They owned most of the land, filled lucrative government jobs, and did not have to pay personal taxes. They did, however, pay indirect taxes. The bulk of the population belonged to the Third Estate, or Estate of Commoners. This ranged from the wealthy middle-classes to wage earners and millions of poor peasants.

Bankruptcy

When Louis XVI came to the throne in 1774, he inherited a debt of four billion livres. As his government's annual revenue (income) was about 500 million livres, he might have managed, with careful housekeeping, to pay off the debt over a number of years. Instead, for five years (1778–1783) France spent most of its revenue supporting the Americans in their War of Independence with Great Britain.

In order to meet the widening gap between revenue and expenditure, the government increased its borrowing and, therefore, its interest payments on the loans. Because these reduced the amount of revenue left to spend, the government had to take out further loans. So the cycle continued until by mid-1788 more than half of France's revenue was going to interest payments and no one was prepared to lend any more. In other words, Louis XVI's government was bankrupt. It was this that triggered the Revolution.

The tax burden of the lower orders: A cartoon from 1789 showing the Third Estate carrying the privileged clergy and nobility.

Taxation

France was one of the wealthiest countries in Europe, and several commercial sectors had prospered during the 18th century. The government had bankrupted itself because it had neither cut expenditure nor increased revenue. Given the high proportion of revenue needed to finance the debt, a significant cut in expenditure was unrealistic.

Higher taxation was the only answer. Successive finance ministers—Turgot (1774–1776), Necker (1777–1781), Calonne (1783–1787), and Brienne (1787–1788)—recognized this but knew that the privileged classes, who paid little or no direct taxes, would be hostile. As the poorer sections of society were already overburdened with taxes, extra revenue could be raised only by cutting back on the tax exemptions of the rich.

Assembly of Notables

In 1787, at the start of what is sometimes called the "pre-Revolution," finance minister Charles Alexander de Calonne proposed a package of reforms that included a land tax and a stamp tax to be paid by everybody.

He also persuaded the king to summon an Assembly of Notables—144 representatives of the nobility—in the hope that they would back his proposals. He reassured Louis that this would not undermine his authority. In a memo to the king in August 1786, he said:

In Assemblies of Notables it is the king who decides matters for discussion. Only matters raised by him may be debated.

Unfortunately for Calonne, the Notables rejected his reforms and the king, siding with them, found a new finance minister, Cardinal Étienne Charles Loménie de Brienne.

Brienne, who had sat in the Assembly, came up with his own set of reforms, including a stamp tax and a land tax, and decided to force them through the *parlements* by a special use of the royal prerogative (or right) known as a *lit de justice*. When the Paris *parlement* objected and said that only an ancient assembly known as the Estates General (which last met in 1614) could vote for new taxes, two of its members were arrested and the others exiled to Troyes, about 106 miles (170 km) southeast of Paris.

The *parlements* and other representative bodies now stirred up widespread protest against "ministerial despotism" (high-handedness). They did so in the name of "liberty," although the only liberties then at stake were those of the privileged few.

The Palace of Versailles, 1722. The magnificent royal palace came to symbolize the vast gulf that separated France's privileged rich from its impoverished masses.

The Vocabulary of Protest

The government then attempted to limit the powers of the *parlements* by issuing edicts to remove their right to confirm new laws and taxes. This united the nobility with other privileged groups in a revolt of the nobility. Members of the Third Estate joined nobles in anti-government disturbances in Paris as well as Dijon, Toulouse, Rennes, and other provincial capitals. France was used to popular protest from the peasant classes, but opposition from all three estates was something new. So was some of the vocabulary—beneath the reactionary banners of the privileged came calls for a complete overhaul of the *Ancien Régime* along lines popular in intellectual circles for the last 50 years.

Watched approvingly by Reason and Truth, the philosopher Jean-Jacques Rousseau (1712–1778) tramples on Error and Lies.

The Enlightenment

The Enlightenment *philosophes* (scientists, philosophers, and writers) were united in the belief that rational, critical observation should be applied in all matters. They condemned political and social practices that appeared irrational, such as inherited privilege, religious superstition, and limits on free trade. The rational basis for government was the welfare of the governed, who had "natural rights." This principle had appeared in John Locke's *Two Treatises of Government* (1690), which justified the setting up of England's constitutional monarchy in the Revolution of 1688–1689.

The Enlightenment's radical ideas, such as Rousseau's stirring declaration in his *Social Contract* (1762),

Man was born free, but everywhere he is in chains.

had penetrated deep into literate French society. It was especially strong among the well-educated bourgeoisie.

These ideas had been reinforced by recent events in America, where Franco–American forces had defeated the British in the name of liberty. As the crisis in France deepened, a growing number of citizens believed that American principles—the right to take up arms against tyranny, equal political rights, no taxation without representation, and the superiority of a republic over a monarchy—were equally relevant in France.

The Estates General

Louis XVI dismissed Brienne in August 1788 and replaced him with a former finance minister, Jacques Necker, who had a popular reputation as a financial wizard. Far more significantly, the king bowed to popular pressure and summoned the Estates General to meet in May 1789.

By summoning the Estates General, the royal government agreed that France should have a say in solving the crisis. However, the Estates General, made up of three houses of 300 deputies each from the Church, nobility, and Third Estate, did not truly represent France. In December 1788, after a widespread campaign opposed by the nobility and clergy, the king again backed down on the question of representation and agreed that the Third Estate could have double representation (600 deputies).

A plate issued to celebrate the opening of the Estates General in May 1789. Hopes that the ancient assembly would be able to solve current difficulties were not fulfilled.

The elections to the Estates General were met with great excitement, tinged with desperation among peasants facing terrible hardship after the bad harvest of 1788. When the Estates General finally met at Versailles on May 5, 1789, deputies presented their electors' complaints and wishes in *cahiers de doléances* ("books of grievances"). Popular expectation ran alarmingly high.

The Divided Estates

Although the Estates General was hopelessly unsuited to the tasks expected of it, its medieval structure focused attention on what was now the central issue: Was the crisis to be solved within the old framework of privilege and legally distinct classes, or was a new government and society required, based on the equality of all citizens? The government gave no lead in this question. Having called the Estates General into existence, it seemed to have no clear idea of what to do with it.

The nobles, who made up the Second Estate, knew exactly what they wanted. Despite the pleas of the Commons (as the Third Estate was also known) that all three Estates should meet together, the nobles decided to assemble and vote as a separate house. A decision by the clergy (the First Estate) to do the same left the Third Estate isolated and technically impotent as its decisions could always be canceled out by the other two. This forced another momentous decision.

A National Assembly

On June 17, 1789, the Third Estate, led by the reformers (or "Patriots"), declared that they were not a single Estate but France's National Assembly, with the sole right to control taxation. Shortly afterward, 150 clerical deputies came to join them. The nobles declared this innovative act both outrageous and illegal.

The Tennis Court Oath: members of the Third Estate swear not to dissolve before they have provided France with a new constitution based upon human rights.

Forging the new constitution, 1789. This optimistic illustration shows the Third Estate, nobility, and clergy working in harmony.

When the king reacted by ordering the closure of the hall in which the self-styled National Assembly met, it adjourned to a nearby tennis court and swore an oath not to dissolve until it had given France a new constitution. Two days later, all three Estates gathered to hear the king's reform program. It was in many ways a remarkable turnabout, granting several of the Patriots' wishes, including equal taxation:

... the king's intention is ... that there should no longer exist any form of privilege or distinction in the payment of public taxation.

Louis also agreed that the Estates General could meet regularly, but he insisted that it continue to do so in the traditional manner, as separate Estates.

The Jurisdictional Revolution

Inadequate reform grudgingly granted from above was not, however, to the Patriots' liking. Only the National Assembly, they argued, could deal with France's needs, and after the king's departure they remained in the hall and continued their discussions. When an official ordered them to leave, the Assembly's president, Jean-Sylvain Bailly, famously replied,

the assembled nation cannot receive orders.

On June 27, the king again relented and told the nobles to sit with the "two other orders." The renaming of the Assembly as the National Constituent Assembly on July 7 completed what is known as France's "jurisdictional revolution."

These events took place against a background of mounting economic distress and rumors of an "aristocratic conspiracy" to overthrow the new Assembly by force. The "Great Fear" was well-founded. When the king had ordered the nobles to join the Assembly, he was merely playing for time.

The astronomer Jean-Sylvain Bailly was hailed as a hero when president of the National Assembly. Later, he became unpopular for allowing troops to fire on a republican mob, and in 1793 he was guillotined (see page 37) as an enemy of the people.

Crisis Point

During the last days of June, the government moved 20,000 troops into the Paris region. Officially, they were there to prevent disturbances and protect the Assembly. However, this did not deceive the deputies, who asked for the soldiers to be withdrawn. Ominously, their request was ignored. The Revolution had reached a critical stage. Up to this point, its events had been brought about by verbal discussion and protest. But now, faced with the muskets and bayonets of reaction, the deputies needed to match force with force or see their gains swept aside.

Stirred up by radical orators, the Paris mob goes on the rampage in its search for food and arms, July 13, 1789.

Bitter Hunger

Bad weather during the summer of 1788, followed by a harsh winter, had caused a severe shortage of grain in the capital. By early 1789 the price of the standard loaf —the staple diet—had almost doubled. During the spring and early summer, starving mobs attacked bakeries, mills, and grain convoys. By July, the mood in the capital was fiery. The English visitor Arthur Young, in his *Travels in France in the Years 1788 and 1789,* reported seeing,

expectant crowds listening ... to certain orators who from chairs or tables harangue their audience. The eagerness with which they are heard and the thunder of applause they receive for every sentiment ... against the present government cannot easily be imagined.

À la Bastille!

Ordinary Parisians seemed almost instinctively aware that the affairs at Versailles, where the Assembly met, touched their lives directly and needed to be supported. The deployment of troops increased their animosity. And when on July 11 the king dismissed Necker, the still popular finance minister, the people decided to act.

A mob attacks the Paris Opera, a symbol of aristocratic luxury, on hearing that the king had dismissed Necker on July 11, 1789.

As in all times of crisis, events acquired a fierce momentum of their own. Street orators whipped up popular fury. Armories and the *Hôtel des Invalides* (the Invalides arsenal) were ransacked for weapons. Soldiers sent to quell the uprising either changed sides or were ordered back to barracks by their worried officers. Then, on July 14, came the cry, *"À la Bastille!"* (To the Bastille!)

Revolution!

The Bastille was a medieval fortress that had served as a state prison since the 17th century. Its importance was symbolic because its prisoners were detained by *lettre de cachet* (royal command from which there was no appeal). In 1789, the Bastille housed only seven prisoners guarded by a small garrison. By 3:30 P.M. on the afternoon of July 14, the mob, now strengthened by the cannon of the local militia (the *Gardes Françaises*), was howling around the Bastille's walls. The commander, realizing he could not hope to resist for long, lowered his drawbridges. The mob entered, and looting and murder continued for several hours. Meanwhile, the electors of Paris set up a revolutionary municipal government (or *commune*), a move followed in 26 other cities. They also formed a National Guard to patrol the streets. When Louis XVI heard of the disturbances, he asked if it was a revolt. No, came the reply: It was a revolution.

Necker, the Swiss-born finance minister whom the king recalled to office after the fall of the Bastille, was unable to control subsequent events. He retired to Geneva the following year.

A romanticized painting of the storming of the Bastille. The walls and towers of the ancient fortress-prison were far less imposing than those shown here.

Starting Point

When did the French Revolution begin? Some say when the king summoned the Estates General, others when the National Assembly was formed, or when the Assembly refused to bow to the royal will. But if a revolution is a swift, fundamental, and permanent change, then surely the fall of the Bastille was the turning point. The changes before that fateful day had certainly been swift. The king's offer of constitutional monarchy at the "royal session" of the Estates General (June 23) had marked a fundamental change in politics. He had agreed, for example, that,

the monies assigned to each ministry will be decided in a regular and permanent manner; the king accepts this general rule even for the monies assigned for the upkeep of the royal household.

Nevertheless, there was still a possibility that a shrewd ministry might use its military resources to quash the revolt. This was no longer conceivable after the people of Paris had set off the counter-coup and seized that most powerful symbol of royal power, the Bastille.

Rudderless

A 15th-century manuscript showing the Three Estates. By 1789, the medieval concept of a society neatly divided in three was centuries out of date.

The events of 1788–1789 developed in a manner no one could see or control. Government bankruptcy produced a moderate reform program that was blocked by vested interests with broad anti-government support. Without thinking things through carefully, the privileged classes then demanded an Estates General. Ironically, this turned popular opinion against them because the Third Estate, rather than the nobility and clergy, was thought to best represent the nation.

By the time the Estates General met, a two-way struggle (king and his ministry versus three Estates) was developing into a three-way one (king and his ministry versus the nobility versus the Third Estate and the lower clergy). After the royal session, the struggle changed again as most of the nobility looked to the king to protect them against the call for equality in taxation and legal status.

This revolutionary cartoon shows the nobility and clergy recoiling in horror as the Third Estate frees itself from its chains.

Peasants and Workers

Flanked by the nobility and clergy, the Third Estate bears the weight of the French world on its shoulders.

There were no peasants or urban wage earners in the Third Estate elected in 1789. Yet it was these people who saved the Assembly. Starving agricultural laborers and the urban poor began rioting in many parts of the country, providing a fearful backdrop for events in Paris and Versailles. If the country had been tranquil, the government would have felt far more confident in taking a stand against its middle-class opponents. Moreover, it was the poor of Paris who had joined with wealthier fellow citizens to storm the Bastille.

By the end of July 1789, several trademarks of the Revolution were in place. It was popular with the great majority of French people. It was controlled by no individual, party, or program but moved in directions that frequently surprised even those most closely involved. It was already radical and was becoming more so by the month. Lastly, and ominously, it had tasted blood and seemed to like it.

CONSTITUTIONAL MONARCHY

August Decrees

By August 1789, the Constituent Assembly (or simply "Constituent") faced two crucial tasks: restoring effective government and drawing up a new constitution. As it was out of the question to use force against rioters still plundering nobles' castles and refusing to meet feudal obligations, it was soon clear that the two jobs would go hand in hand.

The new constitution was put together over the next two years, drastically changing French life forever. Meanwhile, piecemeal legislation made many of the constitution's features effective immediately. The first dramatic steps were taken in the "August Decrees" of 1789 that, among other measures, abolished feudalism and the tithe (national tax) payable to the Church. Since France had long ceased to be a truly feudal country, the former decree was as much symbolic as practical. Personal feudal obligations (such as working the lord's land) were abolished outright, but financial obligations (part of a landlord's income) had to be bought out by those who worked the land with redemption payments. These unpopular charges were abolished in 1792.

The Constituent Assembly abolishes feudalism, August 4, 1789. The nobility were offered substantial compensation for the loss of their traditional financial privileges.

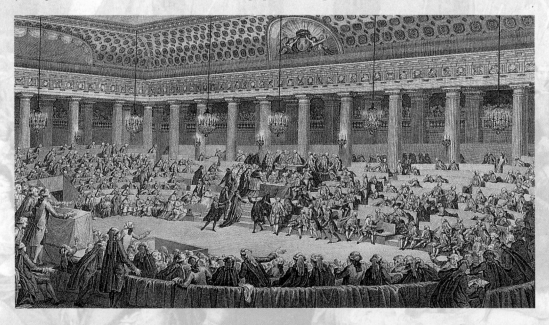

Declaration of Rights

At the end of August, the Constituent set out the principles of its revolution in a "Declaration of the Rights of Man and of the Citizen," which began:

Men are born free and remain free and equal in their rights. Social distinctions can be based only on public utility.

The Declaration established key principles, such as "the nation" being the source of all sovereignty, equality before the law, the right to property, and freedom of speech.

Peasants destroy records of their ancient feudal obligations, such as having to work on their lord's land.

Constitutional Monarchy

In September, the Constituent began to deal with the practical details of France's new constitutional monarchy. It rejected a call for a nominated second chamber and, although accepting the monarch as head of the executive with the power to appoint ministers, the Constituent allowed him the right to veto legislation for, at most, three years. Later, it established property qualifications for voters and office holders. Only the well-off were entitled to be "active" citizens in politics and administration; the rest were "passive" citizens, deprived of the vote and the right to hold office.

By early October, the king had neither accepted nor rejected the Constituent's decrees. A Parisian mob, followed by some troops from the National Guard, marched to Versailles to demand action on bread prices. Although the king sanctioned the August Decrees, the protestors broke into the royal palace and the next day returned to Paris with the royal family. Alarmed, the Constituent followed them to Paris shortly afterward, and on October 21 passed a decree strengthening the powers of authorities responsible for public order.

In November, a new system of local government, including local courts, was introduced based on the division of the country into 83 *départements*, subdivided into districts, cantons, and communes. More controversially, on November 2 the Constituent voted to nationalize Church lands to help pay off the national debt. It was the first of several measures connected with religion that would divide not only the Assembly but the entire nation.

The Declaration of the Rights of Man and of the Citizen. The rights of women, although discussed by a few radicals during the Revolution, were not given legal status in France until the 20th century.

A Bourgeois Revolution

An *assignat*, or government bond, which was supposedly backed by the value of confiscated Church land.

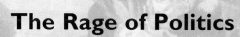

The work of the Constituent is often called a "bourgeois revolution" because it cleared the way for a *laissez-faire* (free market) economy by abolishing restrictive trade practices and organizations. In March 1791, it banned guilds and monopolies and, three months later, it even voted to curb trade unions. Furthermore, existing landowners, both bourgeois and peasant, gained the most when nationalized Church lands were eventually sold. In the meantime, the government sold *assignats* (promises to pay the holder when the Church lands were sold) to finance the Revolution. Soon further *assignats* were printed, raising more money but fueling inflation, and turning *assignats* into a paper currency.

The Civil Constitution

From plenty to famine: a cartoon comparing a plump priest of pre-revolutionary times with a starving one of the 1790s.

In 1790, religion rose to the top of the political agenda. In February the Constituent suppressed many religious orders, and in July a law known as the Civil Constitution of the Clergy was issued to reorganize the Roman Catholic Church. It brought Church structure into line with the new local government divisions and called for bishops and clergy to be elected.

When in November 1790 the clergy were asked to swear an oath of loyalty to the new regime, only seven bishops and about 15 percent of the lower clergy complied. The split spread to the laity, among whom divisions between moderates and radicals were already widening. Tension rose further in the spring of 1791 when the Pope condemned both the Declaration of the Rights of Man and the Civil Constitution of the Clergy.

The Rage of Politics

All this happened in an increasingly politicized country. The removal of censorship had led to the appearance of literally hundreds of new newspapers packed with comments, criticisms, and

The Dominican convent in Paris in which the Jacobin Club originally met.

Robespierre, the lawyer elected to the Estates General in 1789, who became the leader of the most radical elements.

ideas for which direction the Revolution should take next. Political clubs sprang up in Paris, provincial towns and cities, and even in villages. The most influential was the Jacobin Club. Originally broadly based, by mid-1791 it was dominated by the darling of the radicals, Maximilien Robespierre (1758–1794).

Reaction

Outside France, the initial popular reaction to the Revolution had been broadly favorable. The English poet William Wordsworth famously reflected the mood of liberal enthusiasm in "The Prelude" (1850):

Bliss was it in that dawn to be alive,
But to be young was very heaven!

Only hereditary rulers and their close supporters condemned the Revolution from the outset, for obvious reasons. By 1790, however, enthusiasm was waning. There were fears that the common people, not the Constituent, were really in charge of events, a view supported by the stream of *émigrés* fleeing abroad.

Louis XVI was increasingly apprehensive, too. Although he agreed with the new constitution and the Civil Constitution, in October 1790 he authorized exploratory talks with foreign powers about possible intervention to halt the Revolution. His resolve was strengthened by the clergy's hostility to the oath of loyalty. Finally, on June 20, 1791, he tried to flee the country.

An English cartoon depicting the arrest of the fugitive Louis XVI and his family at Varennes in 1792.

The Notables' Dilemma

The king and his immediate family were recognized at Varennes near the Belgian border and brought back to Paris four days later. This put the Constituent in a fragile position. Not only had Louis tried to flee his own country, but he had also, most unwisely, left in Paris his very negative thoughts about the Revolution. The Revolution had brought about, he wrote,

 the destruction of the monarchy, authority ignored, the sanctity of property flouted, the safety of the citizen everywhere endangered, crime unpunished, and total anarchy....

The Constituent had derived from the Estates General. It was made up of men from the "notable" section of society: lawyers, landowners, priests, and a few nobles. They were not democrats in the modern sense: They disliked the Jacobins' radical policies as much as they did the old-style monarchy. Because a constitutional monarch was central to the Constituent's plans, it only suspended Louis' powers until the new constitution was ready. A mass demonstration against reinstating the king, held on July 17 in the *Champ de Mars*, Paris, was forcibly broken up by the National Guard under the leadership of the Marquis de Lafayette, a moderate revolutionary who had fought in America.

The Emerging Radicals

The Champ de Mars massacre brought about a split within the Jacobin Club. The remaining moderates left, leaving radicals like Robespierre and Jérôme Pétion in control. Playing on the fear of a counter-revolution led by monarchists, nobles, and clergy, and supported by *émigrés* and foreign powers, the Jacobins reorganized their network of political clubs and made louder calls for the Revolution to embrace popular sovereignty.

Radical newspapers, such as Jean-Paul Marat's *L'Ami de Peuple* (*The People's Friend*), condemned the new constitution as a bourgeois charade. They called on people to use any means—petitions, demonstrations, even revolt—to obtain their natural political rights. This had obvious appeal to most ordinary people. Had they really embarked on a revolution to replace the rule of the privileged with the rule of the rich?

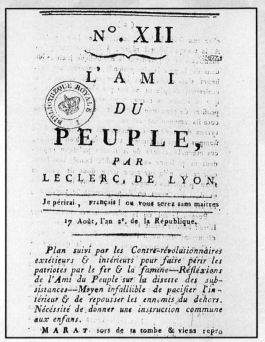

An edition of the radical newspaper *L'Ami de Peuple* produced in Lyon on August 17, 1794. Its founder, Jean-Paul Marat (mentioned at the bottom of the page as "rising from his tomb"), had been murdered the previous year.

The Jacobin leader Jean-Paul Marat, 1743–1793. To avoid arrest, he twice fled abroad and once hid in the sewers of the capital. He was eventually stabbed to death in his bath.

The Legislative

In August 1791 the Constituent, worried about the increasingly hostile attitude toward France in the rest of Europe, gave all *émigrés* a month to return home. The political temperature rose higher when the king of Prussia, Frederick William II, and the emperor of Austria, Leopold II, suggested publicly that armed intervention on behalf of the French king might be necessary.

The new constitution came into effect on September 3, 1791. The king accepted it eleven days later and on October 1, a freshly elected Legislative Assembly (replacing the Constituent) gathered for the first time. Although containing new representatives, the Legislative's membership of "notable" provincial property owners was almost as socially exclusive as the Constituent's had been. But whereas the Constituent had remodeled the country, the Legislative left no permanent institutional or legal changes. Instead, it made its mark in a completely different manner—by taking France to war.

The Legislative Alone

The Legislative, backed by Lafayette and the *Feuillants* (the moderate majority of ex-Jacobins), hoped to stabilize the constitutional monarchy. However, the king's cooperation was essential and since this was not forthcoming at key moments, the Legislative found itself increasingly isolated between conservatives and radicals.

The conservative cause was led by royalists, *émigrés*, and anti-revolutionary Catholics. The radical faction was headed by Jacobins and backed by ordinary citizens, particularly those of the districts of the Paris Commune. They demanded, by force if necessary, a republic without active and passive citizens, and the dispersal of *émigré* forces that were gathering along France's northern border under the command of royalist officers.

Jacques Brissot (1754–1793), who was present at the fall of the Bastille and strongly advocated war with Britain and Austria in 1792. As leader of the Girondins, he was suspected of "bourgeois" moderation and was guillotined the following year.

The Scent of War

After the Jacobin deputy Jacques Brissot (a radical lawyer who had been imprisoned in the Bastille) called for military action against the *émigrés*, the Legislative Assembly decreed that *émigrés* suspected of conspiracy should return home or face death. Three days later, the king vetoed the decree. When in December 1791 he did the same with another decree, the possibility of insurrection increased.

Seriously concerned, the Legislative demanded that the Austrian emperor disperse the *émigrés* gathered in Belgium, which was then controlled by Austria. The Legislative Assembly then nationalized *émigré* property and, in March 1792, forced the king to replace his government with a "Patriot" (or "Brissotin") one led by Charles Dumouriez. The pressure for war was now becoming irresistible. It was desired not just by the Jacobins but also by royalists. They hoped that *émigré* forces, headed by the princes Condé and Artois and backed by the Austrians and Prussians, would defeat the Legislative's forces and so overturn the Revolution.

War and Its Consequences

Leopold II, the brother of Marie Antoinette, Louis XVI's unpopular queen, had formed an anti-revolutionary alliance with Prussia that stopped short of war. However, his death on March 1, 1792, brought his son Francis II to the Austrian throne, and he had no qualms about fighting revolutionary France. Accordingly, on April 20, 1792, war broke out between France and the combined forces of Austria, Prussia, and the *émigrés*. The anti-revolutionary coalition soon crushed a French offensive and planned to advance into France. Panic seized the nation. The war drained resources, inflation soared, and the value of *assignats* fell. The Jacobins used the situation to step up their campaign against the Legislative and the king.

"Young Men Off to Practice Using the Cannon": an image that catches the eagerness with which the revolutionary cause was taken up.

On June 20, after Louis had dismissed Brissotin ministers and vetoed further popular measures, the mob broke into the Tuileries Palace and humiliated him. In July, it was further roused by a government proclamation announcing, "Our native land is in danger."

A manifesto from the Duke of Brunswick, commander of the anti-revolutionary forces, stated that his troops intended to restore the crown's authority and,

> *... if the least violence ... is done ... [to] the Royal Family ... they [the duke's forces] will exact an ever-memorable vengeance ... by delivering the city of Paris to ... total destruction.*

The people of Paris storm the Tuileries Palace and capture the king, August 10, 1792. This act marked the beginning of the end for Louis XVI.

The threat only reinforced the people's determination to defend their Revolution. On August 10, 1792, the people of Paris stormed the Tuileries once more, seized the king (who was imprisoned shortly afterward), and forced the Legislative to suspend the monarchy.

Idealism and Reality

Why did the so-called bourgeois revolution fail? Essentially, its inexperienced leaders were guided by a contradictory mix of self-interest and idealism that was divorced from political reality. Contrast these men with the leaders of the American Revolution. The latter used the experience they had gained in their colonial assemblies to produce (after a false start, the Articles of Confederation) a practical system of government they knew how to operate. Their French counterparts, with little experience of representative government, dreamed up a system founded on abstract and wishful thinking. The American arrangement of checks and balances might have represented an unflattering view of human nature, but it proved far more durable than a constitutional monarchy based on hope.

The Marquis de Lafayette (1757–1834), a reform-minded aristocrat who participated eagerly in the initial stages of the Revolution. After leading the French army to several victories over the Austrians, he went into exile to escape the Jacobins.

The King and the Assemblies

The role played by Louis XVI was obviously crucial. Although no political genius, he was not the dunce he is sometimes made out to be. Nevertheless, like everyone else, he misread the situation at times. He lacked the imagination to realize the scale and the nature of the changes going on around him and consequently, most damaging of all, he failed to establish a working relationship with moderates like Lafayette who might have saved him.

The Constituent and Legislative also lacked political imagination. In particular, they failed to learn the lesson of the fall of the Bastille and the Great Fear: In the summer of 1789, the Revolution had been saved by the ordinary people of France. Understandably, they wanted something in return. Instead, they were prevented from voting or holding office by their poverty, given no opportunity to share in the redistribution of nationalized lands, and when war came they were plagued with severe hardship similar to that of 1789. By 1792, many wondered whether the Revolution had merely replaced an hereditary tyranny with one dominated by the wealthy. It is no wonder, then, that they responded eagerly to the Jacobins' cries that the Revolution had been betrayed.

The Revolution, depicted as a "noble savage" figure, destroys a crowned petty tyrant. The picture suggests the distressing way the Revolution had come to glorify violence.

The Outlook

All this should not detract from the achievements of 1789–1792. The *Ancien Régime* was gone for good. France had been reorganized along lines and on principles that, with a little adjustment, would eventually form the basis of the modern state. But before that could happen, two less welcome features had to be worked through.

The first was war, which was to dramatically shape the remaining years of the Revolution and determine its outcome. A second and related feature was the emergence of the radical left, under the leadership of men like Robespierre and Brissot. Over the next three years this movement probably saved the Revolution, but in so doing, it led it down dark paths that the idealists of 1789 had not even dreamed of. A popular revolutionary song speculated on this future:

The French will always triumph,
Ah! It'll happen, it'll happen, it'll happen!
Despite the traitors, everything'll be ok.
Ah! It'll happen, it'll happen, it'll happen!
We'll hang the aristocrats on lampposts!
Ah! It'll happen, it'll happen, it'll happen!
We'll string up the aristocrats!
Despotism's going to die,
Liberty's going to triumph,
Ah! It'll happen, it'll happen, it'll happen ....

TERROR

The September Massacres

The events of August 10, 1792, are sometimes called the "Second Revolution." The ending of the monarchy (formally decreed on September 21, 1792) was certainly a momentous event, but is probably best seen as marking a new stage in the original Revolution. After all, this was not the first occasion when developments had been determined by the violent intervention of angry Parisians, although this time they were more closely organized by their elected commune.

Half the Legislative's deputies fled the country in the summer of 1792. Those remaining declared their assembly to have lost its mandate and ordered the election by universal male suffrage of a National Convention to produce a republican constitution. Before it met, lawlessness in the capital reached a new and horrific level.

In mid-August, the Prussians advanced across the French border. On September 2 to 6, Paris's *sansculottes* (local political activists), terrified of what might happen if the enemy reached the capital and released its prisoners, established "popular tribunals" in the prisons. After token trials, about half of the city's 2,800 prisoners—royalists and priests as well as common criminals—were killed. They were not executed by the comparatively painless methods of shooting or the guillotine (first used on August 21), but were hacked or stabbed to death.

The Tide Turns

The September massacres horrified the revolutionary leaders. The majority, including Brissot, believed the activities of the *sansculottes* needed to be curbed. Others, notably Robespierre, looked for ways of channeling popular ferocity—interpreted as "the people's will"—to serve their own wills along with the state's.

In the autumn, the tide of the war turned when a revolutionary army defeated the Prussians at Valmy (September 20).

In October, the French advanced into the Austrian Netherlands and offered help to all European peoples struggling against oppression. As a result, on November 27

The French victory over the Prussians at the Battle of Valmy, 1792, marked the turning of the tide in favor of the revolutionary armies.

the captured Sardinian territory of Savoy became a *département* of France.

The Death Penalty

Meanwhile, on September 20, the new National Convention gathered and began its deliberations. One issue dominated: What to do with the king? He was tried on the charge of treason and unanimously found guilty. But there was much disagreement over his sentence. Every deputy spoke to justify his vote. The final verdict, urged by the Jacobins, was 387 in favor of the death penalty, 334 against. In a speech to the Convention on December 3, 1792, Robespierre said:

Yes, the death penalty in general is a crime ... and for this reason ... it may only be justified where it is required by the safety of the individual or of the body politic.... I pronounce this fatal truth with regret ... but Louis must die that the patrie [native land] may live.

Motions for reprieve and for putting the issue to a national referendum were defeated, and on January 21, 1793, "Citizen Capet," as the king of the French was sometimes referred to, went to the guillotine.

So perish all enemies of the Revolution! An executioner shows the crowd the severed head of Louis XVI.

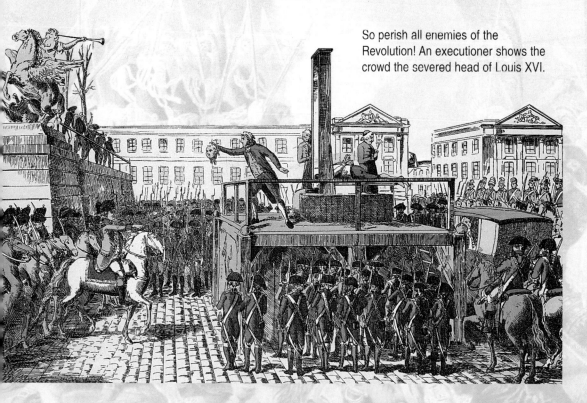

33

Counterrevolutionary forces of the Vendée revolt. Peasant guerrillas included the famous *chouans* (screech owls—so named because of their secret calls), who held out in parts of Brittany and the Vendée until 1799.

Coalition and Revolt

The king's execution settled nothing except the problem of what to do with him. Nonetheless, it did crystallize the situation: Now the revolutionaries could not go back under any circumstances, and most European leaders were convinced that France was in the grip of dangerous populists determined to destroy the existing order.

A hostile international coalition gathered in which Austria and Prussia were joined by Great Britain, the Netherlands, and Spain. War with the great maritime powers and campaigns on five fronts put French forces under immense strain. Before war minister Lazare Carnot reorganized the army, it was driven from the Netherlands and struggled to hold its own elsewhere.

More difficult still, in March a massive revolt broke out south of the Loire River. The Vendée Rebellion was sparked off by a decree conscripting men into the army but it expressed a host of social, political, and religious grievances. Royalist nobles gradually took charge and began forging the rebels into an effective fighting force.

The Convention Divided

All this took place against a background of severe food shortages in the cities, inflation, and another slide in the value of the *assignats*. The Convention attempted to deal with the crisis by measures such as limited conscription, fixing grain prices by a "Maximum" law, and establishing a Committee of Public Safety to oversee general policy.

The Committee's work was severely hampered by divisions among the delegates. The two main groups were the "Mountain," who sat on the Convention's upper benches, and the "Girondins," several of whose members came from the Gironde region. Their antagonism went back to when Brissot (now the most prominent of the Girondins) had called for war in the spring of 1792 and had been opposed by Robespierre (now a Mountain leader). The struggle was primarily about power. Nevertheless, the groups also represented different political attitudes. The Girondins were less willing to give up the liberal values of the early Revolution than the Mountain, which believed that the immediate need to save the Revolution justified short-term harsh and non-liberal measures. This view was in sympathy with the demands of the Paris *sansculottes*, with whom the Mountain forged an unofficial alliance.

The Mountain Coup

The crisis came on June 2, 1793, when a massive crowd, backed by National Guards, surrounded the Convention and demanded the expulsion of the Girondins for betraying the Revolution. When the President of the Convention asked the commander of the guards to end his intimidation, the officer replied,

> *Tell your ****ing President that he and his Assembly can go *** themselves, and if ... [the Girondins] are not delivered, we will blow them all up.*

To make his point, he aimed a cannon at the Convention's doors. Persuaded by the Mountain (and the cannon) that the protest was an expression of the "popular will," the deputies purged 29 Girondins, who were later condemned to death. In addition, 120 of their supporters were also suspended from the Convention. The Mountain was in complete control.

A commemorative plate celebrating the "Mountain" political faction that seized power in June 1793.

The Federalists

Not surprisingly, there was considerable protest from moderates all over France at the *sansculotte*-Mountain purge of the Girondins. Much of this subsided when the Convention pleaded for national unity. Nevertheless, for a variety of reasons armed rebellion broke out in six *départements* in the southeast and southwest, including the great cities of Lyons, Marseilles, and Bordeaux. On August 27, the royalists in Toulon opened the naval base to a British fleet.

The Jacobins (Mountain) condemned the rebels as traitors and "federalists" (i.e., as those who wished to break up the unity of France and therefore destroy the Revolution) and sent armies to crush them. By the end of the year, most resistance, including that of the Vendée, was on its last legs.

Britannia rules the waves—ships of the Royal Navy destroying the French fleet in Toulon after royalists had opened the port to the enemy.

Terror

Meanwhile, the Jacobins in the Convention's key committees (the Committee of Public Safety and Committee of General Security) had come under pressure from *sansculotte*-backed Parisian radicals, like Jacques-René Hébert and Pierre-Gaspard Chaumette, to take stronger action to save the Revolution. The result was a series of measures that instigated a formal policy of "Terror" against perceived enemies. Its chief proponent was Robespierre, who on July 27, 1793, joined the Committee of Public Safety.

The rights that the Revolution had worked to introduce were suspended. A new republican and broadly democratic constitution, which had been accepted in a plebiscite, was put on hold, and the Convention declared that the "provisional" (Jacobin) government would remain in power for the duration of the war. Its dictatorial powers were confirmed in the Law of Revolutionary Government of December 4, 1793, or 14 *Frimaire* Year II (see panel on page 37).

Laws and Victims

A strict law against hoarding food was passed on July 26. On August 23, universal military conscription (the *Levée en Masse*) was introduced.

A revolutionary tribunal in action. The chaotic procedure and dubious impartiality of such tribunals worked against fair trials for the accused.

Some 50 roving revolutionary armies and bands of radical deputies carried the Terror from Paris to the provinces. The Law of Suspects (September 17) gave revolutionary tribunals and commissions wide powers to detain and try anyone believed to hold anti-revolutionary (often interpreted as anti-Jacobin) views. Some 200,000 people were held, of whom 10,000 died in jail and 17,000 were executed (including the queen, Marie Antoinette), most in the Vendée and "federalist" areas. Some *départements*, however, saw almost no executions at all.

The guillotine at work in the Place de la Revolution, 1793. Although it came to symbolize cruel barbarity, the guillotine was adopted in 1791 as a humane method of execution.

The Revolutionary Calendar

On October 7, 1793, the government introduced a new, revolutionary calendar. Year I began on September 22, 1792, the day France became a republic. Each year had 12 months of 30 days each, with names like *Vendémiaire* (vintage: September 22 to October 21). Each month was divided into three ten-day groups with the tenth day a day of rest. The last five days of *Fructidor* (September 17 to 21, the *Sans Culottides*) were holidays. Although used in formal documents, the new calendar was never widely accepted (it reduced the number of holidays considerably!) and was discontinued on January 1, 1806. Dates in this book are given in the traditional form.

No Let-Up

Whatever the rights and wrongs of the Terror, it beat off the reactionary coalition at home and abroad. Despite naval defeats at the hands of the British, by mid-1794 French forces, swelled by the *Levée en Masse*, ably led and fired with nationalist fervor, were dominant almost everywhere.

Military successes did not lead Robespierre and his Committee of Public Safety to relax their grip. After all, Robespierre had declared,

Terror is nothing other than justice, prompt, severe, inflexible.

Opposition from any quarter, left or right, was severely stamped out. In March, a rising of extreme *Hébertists* ended in fresh trials and executions, followed shortly afterward by the elimination of Georges-Jacques Danton and his close supporters—fellow radicals who were now seen as too moderate.

The stream of radical measures continued, too. Slavery was abolished in France's colonies. Other measures, such as taking away the property of detained suspects and altering the procedure of revolutionary tribunals to help the prosecution, appeared vindictive and tyrannical. A few innovations, such as the cult of worship of an unknowable god—the "Supreme Being"—were largely ignored.

The Festival of the Supreme Being, June 8, 1794. Unsurprisingly, the attempt to establish a state-sponsored religious cult was a dismal failure.

Reaction

Finally, after a call for yet another purge of opponents, the Convention had had enough. It denounced Robespierre on July 27 (*Thermidor 9*), and the following day he and 115 of his supporters went to the guillotine. The life of one of the Revolution's most controversial figures had ended: Was he a selfless servant of the downtrodden masses or a tyrant corrupted by power?

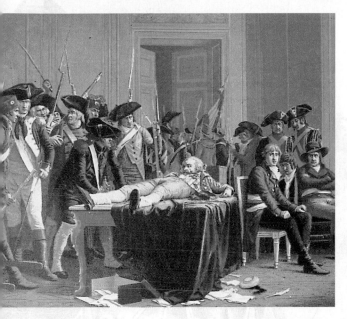

Robespierre after his jaw had been broken by a shot fired by a member of the National Guard, July 27, 1794. He was sent to the guillotine the following day.

As French military victories continued, the Thermidorians (as those who had opposed and removed Robespierre were known) dismantled the machinery of the Terror. By the end of 1794, the Paris Commune and the Maximum Price Law had been abolished, the Jacobin Club was closed, the Committee of Public Safety reorganized, and revolutionary tribunals moderated in favor of defendants. In December, Girondins reappeared in the Convention, which in February 1795 issued a decree providing for freedom of worship and the complete separation of Church and State.

Thermidor

The *sansculottes*, understandably distressed at the turn of events, launched violent protests in April, May, and October 1795. Each came to nothing. The National Guard and the army, now firmly under middle-class Thermidorian control, were more than a match for the leaderless rabble. Besides, the Revolution was clearly no longer in danger. Peace was made with Prussia (April 5), the Netherlands (May 16), and Spain (July 22). The Austrian armies could not match the French, and the British fleet posed little threat to the French mainland.

On August 22, 1795, the Thermidorians approved the Constitution of Year III (the revolutionary calendar was one of the few Jacobin innovations left intact), which restored the principle of only the well-off having the vote. Two months later, after a young officer named Napoleon Bonaparte had put down an attempted Parisian insurrection with "a whiff of grapeshot," the Convention finally dispersed and a new era began.

Counterrevolutionary propaganda: Robespierre, having ordered the beheading of everyone in France, finally guillotines the executioner himself.

The Legacy of the Terror

The Terror tarnished the reputation of the French Revolution forever—and perhaps justifiably. Feeding off Rousseau's idea of forcing people to be free, it brought tyranny in the name of liberty. It romanticized violence and cruelty, dulling people's senses and allowing revenge, envy, and greed to masquerade as virtues. It made a mockery of law and justice. Perhaps, as a distillation and magnification of the faults of the *Ancien Régime*, the Terror was not forward-looking at all.

Revolutionary Shortcomings

Why did the Terror happen? The war, of course, played a vital part in creating the situation in which extremes might appear necessary, even attractive. Yet nations have been successful in war, even against the harshest odds, without resorting to tyranny. So why did France not manage this? Part of the answer lies in the heritage of violence that had dogged the Revolution from 1789 onward. By 1793, the nation had become accustomed to violence, seeing it as the only way to get things done. The ambitions and ruthlessness of key personalities— Robespierre, Danton, Hébert, and others—must also bear a heavy responsibility for what happened.

Loyal Opposition

Just as important was the failure of the revolutionary leaders to establish a constitution capable of channeling the complex and diverse wishes of the nation. Central to this was the revolutionaries' inability to recognize something that had dawned on British and American politicians about eighty years previously: that a political opponent is not, by definition, a traitor. This subtle distinction lies at the heart of democratic and representative government. It was inconceivable under the *Ancien Régime*, and the revolutionary leaders raised in that society carried their limited vision forward into the new era.

As a result, there was no way for differences to be diffused through an opposition and the possibility of an alternative administration. All opponents were seen as "reactionaries," and "enemies of the Revolution"— whether they were royalists, anti-revolutionary clergy, Girondins, *Hébertists*, or simply those unwilling to submit to the "general will" of the *sansculottes*.

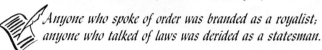

As one Girondin, quoted in the *Memoires* of Antoine-Claire Thibaudeau, a Jacobin lawyer, said:

Anyone who spoke of order was branded as a royalist; anyone who talked of laws was derided as a statesman.

Fruits of Victory

In the end, as we have already seen (pages 38–39), Robespierre and his Jacobins fell because they had outlived their usefulness. Victory undermined the need for, and therefore the acceptance of, extreme measures. Furthermore, the middle-class Jacobins' alliance with the *sansculottes*, the foundation of the Terror, had always been a marriage of convenience rather than a meeting of minds. As the purging of the *Hébertists* showed, the Jacobins backed the *sansculottes* only when it was to their political advantage.

There was also a very practical matter: Many *sansculotte* leaders were shopkeepers and skilled workers who needed to earn a living. There was a limit to the amount of time they could spend on unpaid political activity. By 1795, their energies and pockets had run dry.

The famous "whiff of grapeshot": Artillery commanded by Napoleon Bonaparte disperses the Paris mob in October 1795. "Grapeshot," designed to cause maximum injury, comprised many small pellets of shot that scattered over a wide area.

THE DIRECTORY

A member of the Directory, the five-man executive committee that ran French affairs, 1795–1799. Although criticized for its corrupt and self-serving methods, the Directory provided a period of relative stability after six years of bloody turmoil.

The Directory

Some historians end the French Revolution with the coup of *Thermidor* 9 (July 27, 1794), when Robespierre fell; others choose the coup of *Brumaire* 18 (November 9–10, 1799), in which Napoleon overthrew the Directory (see page 45). This book, however, will focus on the dissolution of the Convention, the last truly revolutionary assembly, on October 26, 1795.

The relatively conservative nature of the new regime was predictable from the general declarations of the new constitution. Gone were the glowing watch words of 1789:

men are born free and with equal rights.

In its place were the far more cautious,

equality consists in having one law for all.

The Constitution of Year III, accepted by plebiscite in October 1795, established a two-house legislature elected on a franchise similar to that of 1791 (see page 23). Elections for one-third of the legislature were annual. Executive power rested with a five-man committee, the Directory, which gave its name to the next four-year period. Besides managing day-to-day affairs, the Directory had wide-ranging emergency powers to curb the freedom of the press and reject the results of elections.

A Troubled Legacy

The Thermidorians had left a troubled legacy. The dismantling of Jacobin economic controls caused considerable (and by now familiar) economic problems: yet another fall in the value of *assignats* and shortages of food and manufactured goods such as soap. A counterrevolutionary White Terror (1795), in which many ex-radicals were killed, left the remaining Jacobins desperate to regain power. The police foiled their most famous attempt, the Babeuf Plot, a forerunner of socialist uprisings, in May 1796.

This cartoon of 1796 shows how the White Terror continued to feed British horror of the Revolution.

At the other end of the political spectrum, royalists and conservatives were furious at a stipulation made by the old Convention. It had said that, whatever the electors decided, for the sake of continuity two-thirds of its deputies were to sit in the new legislature. This stood in the way of the right's hope of recovering power legally and led to an uprising in Paris that was suppressed by the army.

Self-Preservation

The Directory upheld the Constitution of Year III for four years, freely wielding its emergency powers when election results proved unfavorable. Although it successfully managed to steer a middle course between left and right and provided a period of relative domestic stability, it was increasingly seen as self-seeking and corrupt. Moreover, it prevented democratic development because it tolerated little opposition.

A stark example of this intolerance followed the elections of 1797, in which royalists had won. The results prompted the "Coup of *Fructidor* Year V" (September 4, 1797), in which two directors were arrested and the election results in almost 50 *départements* overturned. A severe anti-royalist clampdown closed printing presses and saw numerous arrests.

To the Directory's alarm, their attack on the right gave the left more hope. Neo-Jacobin Clubs appeared, calling themselves "constitutional circles," and the left gained ground in the 1798 elections. Predictably, the Directory organized another purge of the legislature (the "Coup of *Floréal* Year VI": May 11, 1798), this time weeding out their left-wing opponents.

Military Matters

By 1795, France had advanced to its natural frontiers (strategic rivers, mountains, and the sea) by annexing the Austrian Netherlands (Belgium) and the west bank of the Rhine River. Only Britain and Austria remained at war with the Republic. Although France was still unable to match British naval power, it scored further notable victories on land. The most dramatic was General Napoleon Bonaparte's attack on the Habsburg possessions in northern Italy (1796–1797), which forced Austria to make peace at Campo Formio (October 17, 1797).

French success sent a fresh wave of revolutionary fervor across the continent. With French prompting, the people of northern Italy, the Dutch Netherlands, Switzerland, central Italy, and southern Italy established sister republics (named, respectively, the Cisalpine, Batvian, Helvetic, Roman, and Parthenopean republics). All put themselves under French protection. The next plan was to strike at Britain through her possessions in the East. To do this, Napoleon invaded Egypt and defeated the local ruler at the Battle of Pyramids (July 21, 1798). However, he was isolated ten days later when British admiral Horatio Nelson destroyed his fleet and, after an abortive expedition into Syria, he decided to return home.

French troops looting in St. Mark's Square, Venice, 1797. Following the triumph of French armies in the peninsula, many priceless Italian works of art were transported back to France.

The Directory's Troubles

Here, Napoleon found the Directory's popularity ebbing fast. The strain of war and supporting the sister republics had brought further financial difficulties. In response, on September 30, 1797, the Directory had canceled two-thirds of its debts and issued bonds (government promises to pay) in their place. When the value of these bonds fell drastically, the faith of the business classes in the Directory took a similar nosedive.

An all-embracing Conscription Law (September 5, 1798) added to the regime's unpopularity. So did military setbacks following Britain's formation of a new anti-French coalition (1798) that included Russia, Austria, and Portugal. A fresh anti-Catholic campaign didn't help the Directory's popularity, either. Bans on the ringing of church bells were petty but annoying. People were more irritated by the reintroduction (after a brief interlude) of the revolutionary calendar. This meant fewer holidays and the replacement of the traditional Sunday with a new day of rest every tenth day instead of every seventh.

The Revisionist Coup

By the summer of 1799, a group of revisionist (conservative) politicians, led by the director Abbé Emmanuel Joseph Sieyès, decided it was time to replace the Directory and the Constitution of Year III with a system of government that better protected the property reforms and rights of 1789. Needing military backing, they joined with Napoleon, whose failures in the Near East were not widely known.

On November 9, 1799 (*Brumaire* 18, Year VIII), the Revisionists asked the legislature to scrap the constitution. When some deputies objected, Napoleon's soldiers cleared the chamber. After this, the parliamentary coup—known as the *Brumaire* coup—went ahead unopposed. Sieyès succeeded but the real beneficiary was Napoleon, who later recalled,

I listened to everyone's advice but gave advice only when it suited my own interests .... Everyone was caught in my nets.

Hail the conqueror! A romantic portrayal of Napoleon, cheered on by his officers, leaving for the legislature prior to the "revisionist coup" of November 1799.

The port of Marseilles. France's overseas trade was devastated by the naval campaigns of the Revolutionary and Napoleonic Wars, and ports such as Marseilles suffered severe economic depression.

The Directory's Achievements

The Directory has often been dismissed as a sort of impotent stop-gap government between the tyranny of Robespierre and the glories of the Napoleonic era. This may be a harsh judgment. Compared with what had preceded it, the rule of the Directory was stable and tolerant. For the first time since 1788, the French enjoyed an extended period when they knew, more or less, where they stood. They might not have liked the regime, but at least it provided some continuity and stability. Its rule was more balanced than that of its predecessors, too, recognizing local differences and therefore avoiding fresh civil war. Its tolerance is also shown by the fact that, despite its anti-Catholic pronouncements, many *émigré* priests felt it safe to return to France. Finally, after the collapse of the bond scheme, the Directory had some success in putting government finances on a more secure basis.

A Bad Press

The Directory's problem was that these achievements were largely negative—preventing worse things from happening—and so attracted little gratitude from anyone. The regime's middle path left it isolated between genuine democrats, who hated the Directory's self-seeking corruption, and conservatives who were disillusioned with the Revolution and all it stood for.

This isolation influenced later writing, too, ensuring that the Directory had what today would be called "bad press." Left-wing historians and commentators blamed it for betraying the Revolution, while admirers of Napoleon exaggerated its failings in order to justify their hero's participation in the *Brumaire* coup and subsequent seizure of power.

A Pattern Established

Ultimately, like all the Revolution's governments, the Directory failed in that it did not survive. To some extent, it brought about its own downfall. Its fatal mistake was to appoint and support able generals like Bonaparte, Moreau, Brune, and Masséna, but fail to find a way of putting them under civilian command. In so doing, it created a beast like Frankenstein that it could not control. It was significant that by 1799 the success of a purely parliamentary coup depended upon the participation of the army. Now the *sansculottes* were a spent force—the importance of the war had made the military the primary political force in the land.

The Directory's fall completed a pattern, discernible in England's Great Rebellion of 1642–1660, that would repeat itself in revolutions the world over: Popular overthrow of the government led to a period of chaos; this ended when power gravitated to the hands of an organized clique in league with the armed forces; with the military involved in politics, power invariably concentrated into the hands of one man. As Sieyès recognized at once, in France that man was Napoleon:

> *Gentlemen, I perceive that you have got a master. Bonaparte can do, and will do, everything himself.*

Emmanuel Joseph Sieyès (1748–1836), the priest who played a major part in almost every stage of the Revolution. He served in the Estates General and subsequent assemblies, became a director and a consul, was exiled at the Restoration, and finally returned to France in 1830.

THE EMPEROR

Emperor

When the Directory ended, many people regarded the popular young general, Napoleon, as the savior of the Revolution. In some senses this would prove true. Some of its achievements were preserved during his long period of power (1799–1814), and some of the measures he introduced embodied revolutionary ideas. Yet the Revolution's most precious principle—liberty—sank almost without a trace.

The *Brumaire* coup led to the Constitution of Year VIII, which came into effect on December 25, 1799. It was approved by a plebiscite in which three million people voted in favor and four million abstained. Executive power passed to three consuls, of which Napoleon swiftly became by far the most important.

The ambitious First Consul crushed opposition on the left and right. He steadily tightened censorship and used the police to watch potential opponents. In 1802 he was made consul for life, again confirmed by plebiscite (a device that invariably supports the regime in power). On December 2, 1804, he was declared Emperor of the French and was crowned by Pope Pius VII in Notre Dame Cathedral, Paris.

King to emperor—the Revolution comes full circle: Pope Pius VII crowns Napoleon and Josephine Emperor and Empress of France.

Reform and Reaction

Napoleon's domestic policy was a curious mixture of the forward-thinking and the cautious. His overhaul of the French legal system with a new Civil Code (1804), Code of Civil Procedure (1806), and Penal Code (1810) was, like the Revolution's abolition of feudalism, a reform that enlightened thinkers had long been calling for. The establishment of a Bank of France and the stabilization of the economy were universally welcomed, especially by the Revolution's middle-class ex-leaders. Educational reforms, such as the establishment of *lycées* (1802)—secondary schools open to all able pupils—in some ways harked back to the Convention's radical plans for transforming French education.

On the other hand, Napoleon admitted that his religious Concordat with Pope Pius VII (1801) and the abolition of the revolutionary calendar were necessary simply to boost the authority of the civil power:

In religion I see not the mystery of the Incarnation but the mystery of the social order.

They were part of a process that included putting down the last rural revolts, reorganizing local government along lines similar to those of the *Ancien Régime*, and granting an amnesty to *émigrés* (1802).

Austerlitz: the "Battle of the Three Emperors." Napoleon, outnumbered and outgunned, crushed the combined armies of Emperor Alexander I of Russia and Emperor Francis II of Austria.

Master of the Continent

People overlooked the contradictions in Napoleon's domestic policies because of his triumphs abroad. For a decade, French supremacy was challenged only by Britain's money and its Royal Navy. By 1802, when peace was made with Britain at Amiens, Napoleon had reestablished French power in northern Italy and forced Austria to come to terms at Lunéville (1801). He smashed Britain's third anti-French coalition with a remarkable victory over the Russians and Austrians at Austerlitz (1805). When Prussia joined the coalition in 1806, Napoleon overwhelmed it at Jena-Auerstadt and entered Berlin. Finally, after beating the Russians at Friedland in 1807, the Treaty of Tilsit left him master of the continent.

A New Royalty

Even before becoming emperor, Napoleon had established a new aristocracy with his Legion of Honor (1802)—a band of citizens, with Napoleon at its head, rewarded with titles for outstanding service. Two years later, he revived the title Marshal of France for his greatest generals. In 1806, he acquired the power to grant hereditary lands. The Bonaparte dynasty expanded when Napoleon made his elder brother, Joseph, king of Spain (1808). He then pushed the hereditary principle further by divorcing the Empress Josephine, who had failed to give him a son, and marrying the Archduchess Marie Louise of Austria. Their son would be given the title "King of Rome" and made heir to the French Empire.

In 1805, 1807, 1810, and 1811, censorship was further tightened in an attempt to quiet rumbles of discontent. Good relations with the Pope fell apart in 1809, when France occupied the Papal States. Pius VII excommunicated the emperor and was arrested a month later. Although Pius was pressured into making a new agreement in 1813, he later withdrew his signature.

The Continental System

The Treaty of Tilsit with Russia and Prussia was the high-water mark of the Napoleonic adventure. The British naval victory at Trafalgar (1805) had dimmed the emperor's aura of invincibility, and the following year he hit upon a new strategy for defeating his old enemy: commercial warfare. His Continental System banned all trade between continental Europe and Britain, the "nation of shopkeepers."

The embargo certainly caused Britain hardship, but it also hit European merchants and manufacturers, swelling anti-French discontent. This was most noticeable in Spain, where British forces and native guerrillas tied down large numbers of French troops. Austria, encouraged by events in the Iberian peninsula, briefly broke ranks in 1809 but was defeated at Wagram. Russia was next to desert, prompting a massive French invasion in 1812 that resulted in the loss of almost half a million Frenchmen.

Admiral Nelson's destruction of the Spanish and French fleets at Trafalgar (October 21, 1805) made invasion of Britain an impossibility. It also created a stalemate, with France dominant on land and Britain supreme at sea.

The retreat from Moscow, November 1812. French forces stream over hastily constructed wooden bridges across the icy Berezina River.

Exile

The defeat in Russia was the beginning of the end. Napoleon may have recognized this, for during his disastrous retreat from Moscow he summed up his position with his favorite phrase:

From the sublime to the ridiculous there is but a single step.

The end at last: Napoleon on the deck of HMS *Bellerophon*, the British warship that transported him to exile on the remote St. Helena.

Prussia, Sweden, and Austria now joined Britain and Russia in yet another anti-French coalition. While British forces invaded France from the south, their allies decisively defeated Napoleon at the Battle of the Nations (Leipzig, 1813) and occupied Paris. On May 3, 1814, Napoleon was exiled to the island of Elba.

The former monarchy was restored. However, the French rapidly became disillusioned with the unimpressive Louis XVIII and gave their emperor a glorious welcome when he fled captivity and returned home in March 1815. The glory was short-lived. Napoleon had some initial success against British and Prussian forces, but was soundly beaten at Waterloo on June 18. He surrendered to the British and, four months later, his vanquishers exiled him again—this time to the remote Atlantic island of St. Helena, where he died in 1821.

Heir to the Revolution?

The French painter David's dramatic depiction of Napoleon crossing the Alps during his invasion of Italy.

As consul, Napoleon had announced that the Revolution was over and that he would now consolidate its achievements. In 1812, he declared with obvious pride:

The greatest lords of the old regime now dine with the revolutionaries. My government has created this union.

There are three ways to look at Napoleon's claim. First, he really had fused the best of the old world and the new. Next, he had betrayed the Revolution by imposing a new tyranny. And finally, his government was the natural outcome of the Revolution, cementing its principles in strong and effective government.

Political Liberty

The first of the Revolution's three popular principles was liberty. As it meant different things to different people, it was the most difficult to define. To the bourgeoisie, for example, it meant freedom from government interference in their pursuit and use of wealth, under a government of their own choosing. To the *sansculottes*, on the other hand, it meant freedom from poverty as well as the right to participate in politics.

The Parisian bourgeoisie enjoying the spring sunshine after the Peace of Amiens (March 25, 1802) had brought a brief respite from the war.

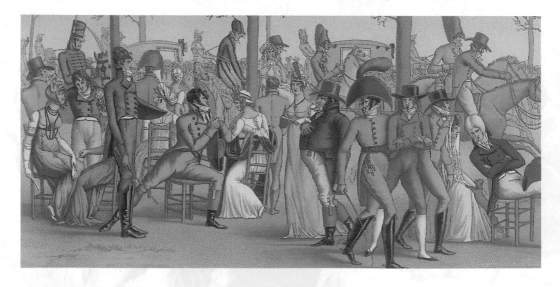

In its simplest political form, liberty meant freedom from the sort of unregulated power wielded by the monarchy in the *Ancien Régime*. This implied some sort of representative and responsible government. The requirements of war had ensured that such liberty was short-lived. It was wounded by the Terror, stifled under the Directory, and finally killed by Napoleon. A soldier accustomed to giving orders, he completed the process by which the political freedoms dreamed of in 1789 were gradually worn away.

Stability Before Liberty

No compromise: a revolutionary poster that reads, "The Republic's undivided unity: Liberty, Equality, and Fraternity—or death." Was Napoleon really the defender of these values?

True, Napoleon used the plebiscite to confirm his power, but this was no substitute for representative government. Assemblies were subject to his will, and opposition was muzzled by censorship. There was no point in his claiming on St. Helena that had he triumphed in 1812, he would have become a constitutional emperor. To do that would have required setting aside all the steps he had taken to establish a long-lasting, hereditary Bonaparte dynasty.

This does not mean that people generally disapproved of Napoleonic rule. Quite the contrary. In the eyes of many French men and women, the quest for liberty had brought nothing but turmoil, dissent, and bloodshed. As a result, they were willing to sacrifice liberty for stability, as long as it was accompanied by a degree of equality and prosperity.

Where freedom was concerned, therefore, Napoleon's rule was two-faced, both denying and concluding the Revolution. His imperial power was the opposite of the revolutionary principle of political liberty. At the same time, his rule was both understandable and generally welcome: a natural reaction to the Revolution's failure to put its principles into practice. In simple, human terms, by 1799 freedom from civil disturbance was more acceptable than freedom to participate in the political process.

Equality

The second of the Revolution's key principles, equality, fared better under Napoleon. As he boasted (page 52), great lords and revolutionaries did indeed eat together, or at least they competed on equal terms for the emperor's favor. Most careers were open to talented individuals with education. This meant that the great mass of illiterate peasantry had little chance of advancement, but it was a considerable improvement on the *Ancien Régime*. The Civil Code (or *Code Napoléon*) consolidated many revolutionary achievements and principles, although the secondary status it gave women highlighted its conservatism.

Against this must be placed Napoleon's undemocratic rule and the appearance of the Legion of Honor. The new Napoleonic aristocracy ran contrary to the principle of equality. Neither was there any attempt to follow the Revolution's first hesitant steps toward greater economic equality. But at least under the Consulate and Empire the country prospered, helped by measures such as the establishment of the Bank of France. Moreover, this wealth was more widely distributed than under the old regime.

The first edition of the Civil Code of French Law (known as the *Code Napoléon*), a logical measure that reformers had been calling for since the early 18th century.

Napoleon awards Crosses of the Legion of Honor in the Church of the Invalides, Paris. By 1814 there were 32,000 members of the Legion, most of whom had served in the army or navy.

Pope Pius VII (1742–1823), who signed the 1801 Concordat with Napoleon but fell out with him when Rome was incorporated into the French Empire (1808). Pius subsequently spent six years under arrest.

Fraternity

Fraternity, or brotherhood, was always the most obscure of the revolutionary principles. Significantly, the constitution of 1799 substituted "property" in its place. Nevertheless, Napoleon did manage in large part to restore social harmony and heal old wounds. Important steps along this path were the Concordat with the Pope, the suppression of Jacobinism for undermining the common good, and granting an amnesty to royalists willing to support him.

Child of the Revolution?

So how did the revolutionary legacy fare in Napoleon's hands? On St. Helena, when he was making a conscious effort to secure his reputation for posterity, he declared himself to have been,

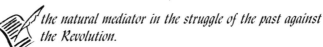

the natural mediator in the struggle of the past against the Revolution.

To some extent this was true, although the conflict between the Revolution and the *Ancien Régime* was less important than the conflict within the Revolution about what form it should take. More useful is Napoleon's insistence that he threw out revolutionary theories (ideology) but preserved revolutionary interests (practical gains). Certainly, cries of "liberty, equality, and fraternity" were not welcomed under the Empire, but Napoleon did safeguard the Revolution's redistribution of lands and legal gains. Yet that is only part of the story.

"Liberty" was more than just theory—it involved political rights and an elective system of government based on those rights. So in getting rid of liberty (and a good deal of equality) Napoleon was rejecting both practical gains and ideology. This made him less a child of the Revolution than a ruler in the style of an 18th century "enlightened despot," such as Austria's Joseph II or Frederick the Great of Prussia. The essence of the Revolution, as seen in the events of July 1789, was that the people knew best. The essence of Napoleonic rule was that the emperor knew best.

RESTORATION

CHAPTER SIX

A cartoon of the victorious allied heads of state after the final defeat of Napoleon in 1815. They are (left to right) Alexander I of Russia, Louis XVIII of France, George III of Britain, and Francis II of Austria.

Restoration

There is no obvious point when the Revolution ceased to have a major influence on French society and politics. The fall of Napoleon might have been a suitable point had not the Empire and restored former monarchy overlapped in 1814–1815. Furthermore, the Revolution had by then become the pivot around which all recent French history turned. The very term "restoration" made no sense without reference to it.

The restoration of the monarchy by the victorious Allies after the defeat of Napoleon in 1814 was not inevitable. Had the emperor been prepared to abandon his empire, the Allies might have let him remain ruler of France. But he was too consumed by his own egotism to accept such a compromise and was exiled, returned for his "Hundred Days" (actually 110), then exiled for good.

The Charter

The French showed their verdict on the First Restoration, introduced while Napoleon was on Elba, by the joy with which they greeted their returning emperor. His second defeat, however, meant that the monarchs were there to stay. Louis XVIII and his advisors faced a broad range of constitutional possibilities. These ranged from an *Ancien Régime*-style monarchy to a constitutional monarchy along the lines of 1791. The king, deeply conservative, was inclined toward the former but had sufficient political sense to realize it was unacceptable. The result, which he granted to his people in 1814 in the form of a charter, was a compromise.

Like so many of the monarchs' pre-revolutionary policies, the Charter was ill-conceived. It took the form of a sort of mixed selection of pre-revolutionary,

Delighted French citizens welcome their charismatic emperor on his return from exile on Elba, 1815.

revolutionary, directorial, and Napoleonic features. Louis' sense of divine right came straight from the *Ancien Régime*. This is well illustrated by the following exchange; never once—even when in exile—had the king stopped believing he was God's appointed gift to the French people:

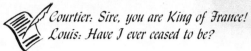

Courtier: Sire, you are King of France!
Louis: Have I ever ceased to be?

Enduring Divisions

The Charter's opening references to liberty and equality and the talk of representative government harkened back to the heyday of the Revolution. The promise of a free press, but with the government able to censor it if this freedom was abused, seemed like the double-talk of the Directory. Finally, most importantly in the eyes of many people, the papal Concordat and freedom of religion, the Civil Code (including the principle of equality before the law), and the promise of careers open to talent were retained from Napoleonic times. To add to the confusion, the relationship between the executive, headed by the king, and the two houses of the legislature was unclear. In some ways, this muddled situation was to be expected. The different features of the new constitution and the uncertainty at its heart only mirrored the diversity that the Revolution had created within the nation at large.

Louis XVIII in his office. Was this picture intended to give the impression that the king, like his predecessor Napoleon, was prepared to work for his people?

Reaction

At first glance, the restoration of Louis XVIII looked like a triumph for the anti-revolutionaries. The Charter of 1814 declared that,

The King's person is inviolable and sacred ... [and] the King is the supreme head of state.

It may be argued, however, that such backward-looking language was less significant than it seemed.

Before the meeting of the Estates General in 1789, the nation's hopes, wishes, and fears had been set out in numerous *cahiers de doléances* (see page 15). Careful analysis of these shows that the vast majority of people did not hope for a revolution. Instead, they wanted reform and an improvement of their economic status.

This may not be surprising. France was, and probably still is, a deeply conservative country. The calling of so ancient an institution as the Estates General expressed a wish, however vague, for a return to a better past. At the time of the Revolution 90 percent of France's population lived in small towns and villages and made their living, directly or indirectly, from agriculture. Most could not read or write. Their true concerns were not with abstract ideas such as equality or constitutions, but with far more fundamental matters: the harvest, the price of bread, taxation. The Revolution had done little to alter any of this.

The peasants' life: Although the Revolution focused attention on the militant wage earners and bourgeois people of Paris, the great majority of French people lived in rural communities that depended on agriculture.

With this in mind, the developments in France during the twenty years 1795–1815 are more easily understood. Despite the excesses in Paris and a handful of other large cities, in the countryside there was more continuity than discontinuity. Nor were changes in government policy, from economic liberalism to the close state regulation of the Maximum, as radical as they appeared. Most had their forerunners in the *Ancien Régime*.

Napoleon, too, was in many ways a conservative figure—a kind of super-efficient king. He provided a traditional figurehead in the same way as the Supreme Being replaced the Christian God during the Revolution's most radical phase. The people needed and wanted symbols that linked them to their past. The restoration of Louis XVIII fits into this pattern.

Most peasants had never been much interested in political theories. An ordinary family in Burgundy, Provence, or the Tarn was not unduly concerned whether the government in Paris was in the hands of a committee, a consul, an emperor, or a king. What did matter was how that government, through its local officers, affected their lives. After nearly a generation of warfare that killed one and a half million young Frenchmen, they would look favorably on almost any regime that brought peace. In this context, the restoration was less a final defeat for the Revolution than another attempt to solve the problems it had raised.

Two 18th-century washerwomen and a peasant. The daily lives of ordinary people like these were not greatly changed by the momentous events of 1789–1815, although their economic situation probably had deteriorated.

A NEW FRANCE

The Tragic Paradox

*It was the best of times, it was the worst of times,
it was the age of wisdom, it was the age of foolishness.*

A cartoon by the British satirist James Gillray (1757–1815), a sworn enemy of all falsehood, ironically entitled "The Zenith of French Glory; the Pinnacle of Liberty, Religion, Justice, Loyalty, and all the Bugbears of Unenlightened Minds, Farewell!" It depicts the Revolution as a vulgar harbinger of intolerance and cruelty.

With a novelist's insight, Charles Dickens presented the tragic paradox of the French Revolution in *A Tale of Two Cities* (1859). Launched by men of ideas, it led to the seizure of power by a man (Napoleon) who openly despised intellectuals. Intended to bring about representative and responsible government, it enabled orators and tyrants to exercise greater power than that ever wielded by a French king. The willingness to turn to a charismatic leader in times of trouble remained a feature of French political life for many years to come.

In the name of liberty, fraternity, and peace, the Revolution fractured France and brought untold misery, destruction, and bloodshed. Thousands fled abroad. Schools and hospitals closed. Palaces, churches, monasteries, and manors were looted and roads allowed to fall into disrepair. The Terror accounted for the death of thousands of people, the Revolutionary and Napoleonic Wars for well over a million more.

Furthermore, although the Revolution proclaimed the rights of the downtrodden and oppressed, it brought greatest misery to the poor. It is estimated that 60 percent of the victims of the Terror were peasants and wage-earning workers. The collapse of the aristocratic way of life led to massive unemployment among the servant class. The war ruined the economies of great ports such as Marseilles. By 1798, there were around 60,000 unemployed in Paris, equivalent to about one-tenth of the city's population.

*The Zenith of French Glory; _The Pinnacle of Liberty.
Religion, Justice Loyalty, & all the Bugbears of Unenlightend Minds, Farewell !*

Rational improvement: The standard meter, the basic unit of the new metric system, was put into place at the Petit-Luxembourg, Paris, in 1799.

Centralization

In other areas, too, the Revolution's consequences were the opposite of those intended. Starting as an anti-government protest, it led to a significant increase in the power of the government to interfere in people's daily lives. This showed itself in measures such as conscription and the Maximum.

By 1794, the number of central government employees had risen almost ten-fold. This was not necessarily unwelcome. It provided employment and was part of the process of untangling the chaotic administration of the *Ancien Régime*. The reorganization of the country into *départements*, the imposition of the metric system, and the new Civil and Penal Codes were part of the same process. They were all significant steps in the development of a centralized modern France.

The Feeling of Betrayal

Heralded as a popular movement, the Revolution was soon most strongly opposed by the common people. It has been suggested that even the *sansculottes*, by opposing the Revolution's economic liberalism, were in a sense anti-revolutionary. Of course, individual experiences varied widely, depending on local circumstances. Nevertheless, the general sense was that between 1790 and 1795 the traditional foundations of people's lives had been shaken. It was not what they had intended, and they did not like it.

A *sansculotte* wearing the tattered trousers that gave him his name. The term "sansculotte" meant "without knee-breeches," the dress of the bourgeoisie. From 1792–1794 *sansculottes* also referred to a specific group of radical activists who sided with the Jacobins.

Peasants attacking an aristocratic château during the Revolution. Such action brought short-term gain in the form of loot; however, the closure of many châteaux and other institutions of the *Ancien Régime* caused widespread unemployment.

A romantic painting of *émigrés* fleeing France to escape the Revolution. Although most *émigrés* were from the noble or bourgeois classes, their number included many ordinary working people.

Noble Hardship

Proportionally, the two groups that the Revolution hit hardest were the First and Second Estates, the clergy and the nobility. Although the calling of the Assembly of Notables had foreshadowed the Revolution, and men like the Marquis de Lafayette had been among its keenest early leaders, the nobility suffered grievously. Their châteaux were sacked and hundreds were executed by revolutionary tribunals of one kind or another.

Perhaps 20,000 nobles fled abroad to save their lives, leaving most of their possessions at the mercy of the revolutionaries. (One-third of registered *émigrés*, incidentally, were peasants or workers.) As a result, some 12,500 noble families lost some or all of their land. The compensation paid to office-holders who lost their positions was hardly generous and was undermined by inflation. Nevertheless, a number of aristocrats managed to buy back a substantial proportion of their lands and, by Napoleonic times, they were once again among the wealthiest in France.

Relics of a Bygone Age

Yet a deeper, less obvious change had occurred. Despite the eventual return of the monarchy, members of the old nobility continued to suffer the effects of insults and indignities brought on by the loss of their titles and hereditary position in society. The very word "aristocrat" had been the radicals' most widely-used term of abuse. In 1826 the Count de Villèle would complain,

The bonds of subordination are so loosened everywhere ... the evil is in our mores [customs], so influenced are we still by the Revolution.

As de Villèle recognized, the Revolution had destroyed the mystique of hereditary aristocracy. In the post-revolutionary world in which careers were more or less open to talent, the old nobility largely stood aside from politics. They survived, often wealthy and sometimes still revered, but essentially curious relics of a past age.

The Sufferings of the Church

The Revolution's effect on the Church was broadly threefold. Clergymen themselves suffered. About 1,200 died and a further 25,000 emigrated. These included half of the country's parish priests. Monasticism disappeared for a time and never recovered its former importance.

The dramatic cut in the number of clergy, along with clerical poverty following the abolition of tithes and the sale of Church lands, had a serious effect on the Church's social operations. Hardest hit were education and care of the poor and sick. Attempts by revolutionary governments to plug the gap were either never realized or inadequately funded. Consequently, throughout France basic literacy declined and large numbers of the sick and destitute were left without treatment or relief.

Finally, the 1801 Concordat made the French Church a department of state, but kept the Pope as its spiritual head. Although the Concordat distressed many clergy, it left the Church free from political and commercial distractions and therefore more able to concentrate on its spiritual activities.

A cartoon showing a priest preaching to his new congregation of farm animals and threatening them with hellfire for their sins. His human audience has deserted him, liberated from priestly superstition by the secular teachings of the Revolution.

The French Economy

During the 18th century, despite expansion in overseas trade, especially with the colonies, the French economy had faced considerable difficulties. War had brought disruption and inflation. Agricultural production had been relatively stagnant and there had been periodic famines. Urban workers' wages had not kept up with inflation, and manufacturers had been slow to adopt the new industrial processes appearing in Britain, France's principal commercial rival. Added to this was the severe economic downturn in 1787 to 1789, as well as the weak economic outlook even before the Revolution. Sadly, however, despite expectations to the contrary, the impact of what followed only made things worse.

Inflation

The ending of feudal dues failed to benefit tenants, because landlords simply raised rents to compensate for lost income. The breakup of great aristocratic and clerical households meant thousands of servants were suddenly without work. Similarly, the ending of provincial *parlements* and estates in 1789 deprived towns of employment and income. The consequent unemployment bred poverty, vagrancy, and crime.

Poor relief, *Ancien Régime*-style: Economic disruption, inflation, and high taxation caused widespread poverty among the urban and rural poor through the revolutionary period.

NE POUR LA PEINE

Born to suffer: a late 18th-century engraving of a poverty-stricken peasant. Sadly, after all the upheaval of the Revolution, such people ended up no better off.

The situation was made worse by the currency manipulation associated with the issuing of _assignats_, which were supposed to be backed by confiscated land. By 1797, paper money worth nearly 45 thousand million francs had been issued, which was around seven times the market value of the land. The inflation and uncertainty to which this gave rise had a serious impact on the value of wages, as a Paris police report of January 1794 indicates:

The price of poultry goes up every day—it has doubled in a fortnight. Eggs are so expensive that no one can touch them now.

Enterprise suffered, too. Debtors delighted at the falling value of what they owed. Creditors despaired of seeing a return on their money and were reluctant to invest further. In such uncertainty, only the foolish or desperate were prepared to put capital into new businesses. Britain's industrial development left France struggling in its wake, and French agriculture remained stuck with its often rather old-fashioned practices.

The Effect of the War

On top of all this came the war. Some sectors (arms producers, uniform manufacturers, and providers of army supplies, for example) inevitably did well. Conscription helped lower unemployment, too. But for the sector of the economy that had previously been most buoyant—overseas trade—the wars spelled disaster.

The instrument of France's undoing was Britain's Royal Navy. Its victories in battle ensured that by Trafalgar (1805), British merchants had a free run of the world's oceans and British soldiers could be shipped overseas at will. In seven years, the British blockade of French ports reduced the proportion of the French national income derived from overseas trade from 25 to 9 percent.

In response, France increased its trade with continental Europe. It also received massive wealth in loot and taxes from occupied territories. But this was short-term relief and did little to compensate for the deep-seated economic disruption caused by the Revolution.

The Triumph of the Bourgeoisie

A typical Parisian bourgeois family in the early 19th century. Such people benefited from the *laissez-faire* economic policies that became the norm after 1789.

The Revolution did not bring hardship to every group in French society. As leaders of the Revolution, the bourgeoisie were particularly successful. They retained the right to vote. With the education, contacts, and confidence to take advantage of the situation, they flourished when careers were opened to talent. The era of the bureaucrat, businessman, and professional man was dawning. In short, enriched through the purchase of noble and Church land, the bourgeoisie had emerged as a new property-owning elite.

Another group to do well were career soldiers. As the emperor himself showed, the army was one of the few professions in which an able man could rise from relatively obscure origins to great power and riches. Protestants, although subjected to periodic outbursts of "White Terror," benefited from the state's acceptance of religious toleration. Jews, too, felt some measure of relief.

Racial and Sexual Equality

The Assembly and Legislative passed measures that edged toward racial equality. Finally, in 1794, the Convention abolished African slavery in the colonies and accepted all colonial males as full citizens. By this time, however, the blacks of Saint-Domingue (the world's richest colony) had risen in revolt. Restored to loyalty by the 1794 decree, they broke away again when Consul Napoleon restored colonial slavery in 1802. Two years later, they established the fully independent republic of Haiti. Elsewhere, slavery remained a stain on French colonial life until 1848.

To modern eyes, the Revolution's failure to extend its promise of equality to women is surprising, particularly since they had played such a key role in episodes such as the march to Versailles in October 1789. They joined revolutionary groups, set up clubs of their own (banned in 1793), and were prolific writers of revolutionary pamphlets. Of the several that called for female emancipation, Olympe de Gouges' *The Rights of Women and the Citizen* (1791) is perhaps the most memorable:

Sisters of the Revolution: Working-class women march on Versailles, 1789. Although women played a significant part in the Revolution, they remained second-class citizens throughout the 19th century.

Article 1
Woman is born free and lives equal to man in her rights. Social distinctions can be based only on the common utility.

The Vocabulary of Hope

De Gouges' plea was ignored, but it was not in vain. Like many of the Revolution's idealistic pronouncements that came to nothing in the short-term, it created a new political vocabulary of hope. This, in the long run, was perhaps the Revolution's most enduring legacy for France (and elsewhere). The Revolution's lasting practical achievements—the abolition of feudalism, religious toleration, codification of the law, and abolition of hereditary privilege—had been foreshadowed during the *Ancien Régime*. Its rhetoric, on the other hand, went much further. Democracy and full rights for all —male and female, black and white—were not achieved, but at least they were now on the agenda. That, perhaps, made all the misery and violence a little more tolerable.

Olympe de Gouges (1745–1793), the poorly educated butcher's daughter who challenged the male leaders of the Revolution to introduce female rights. Outspoken in her opposition to revolutionary violence, Olympe was guillotined during the Terror.

THE MOTHER OF REVOLUTIONS

New Warfare

The impact of the French Revolution extended far beyond politics. The Revolutionary and Napoleonic Wars, for example, marked a significant change in the way wars were fought. Up to this point, European warfare had been conducted by relatively small armies in limited circumstances. The Committee of Public Safety's *Levée en Masse* started the idea of mobilizing a whole population for national defense. The principle of the *Levée* was adopted elsewhere, making warfare throughout Europe into an activity that embraced the whole nation. It meant not just vast armies, but gearing a nation's economy and taxation system to maintain them. Britain's progressive income tax (1799) was one important consequence. Another was reinforcement of the link between war and growing nationalism.

Winners and Losers

Despite France's many victories, in the long run it was its enemies that gained politically. In 1815, France returned to its natural frontiers. Its principal continental rivals, Prussia and Austria, emerged from the wars more powerful and more united. Russia confirmed that it was now a major force in European politics. Britain, humiliated by American independence in 1783, had laid the foundations of almost a century of world dominance. On the other hand, some states (most notably Poland, 1795) disappeared altogether in the turmoil. So did that relic of a bygone age, the Holy Roman Empire (1806).

Nationalism

Perhaps the Revolution's most potent export was nationalism. For the French it proved a double-edged sword. Wherever the French armies advanced—into Italy, the Netherlands, Germany, and elsewhere—they carried with them the ideology of the Revolution and their love of *la Patrie* as expressed in the opening words of the *Marseillaise*, adopted as the French national anthem in 1795:

A patriotic portrayal of the composer of the *Marseillaise*, Claude Joseph Rouget de Lisle (1760–1836). Despite its aggressive lyrics, it remains the French national anthem.

General José de San Martin (1778–1850), the Argentinean who played a major part in the revolutions against Spanish rule in Argentina, Chile, and Peru (1812–1821). He developed his ideas while living in Europe, 1785–1811.

Let's go, children of our native land,
The day of Glory is here.
Tyranny stands against us,
The bloody flag is raised ...

The anthem was banned by Napoleon and Louis XVIII, later revived and banned again, then finally reinstated for good in 1879.

Patriotism proved as infectious as revolutionary ideas, particularly in areas like northern Italy that were united by French arms. The consequent flowering of nationalism helped turn local populations against the invader. Its effects were felt even in reactionary Austria and Russia, where in 1809–1812 calls for volunteers to fight the French produced tens of thousands of recruits. Wartime nationalism also prepared the ground for the German and Italian unification movements of the next 75 years.

The heady draft of nationalism worked its fiery magic further afield, too. The first continent to feel its effects was South America, where freedom from Spanish and Portuguese masters was brought on by the Napoleonic invasion of the Iberian peninsula. It was from France rather than the United States that the leaders of the Latin-American independence movements drew much of their language of rights and popular sovereignty.

Two Revolutions

The worldwide legacy of the French Revolution cannot be separated from that of the preceding American Revolution. Together they gave the oppressed a vocabulary of hope: "No taxation without representation"; "Liberty, Equality, and Fraternity"; "All men are created equal"; "The rights of man." These heady phrases, translated and refined, became the watchwords of campaigners against tyranny for all subsequent generations.

However, while sharing similar vocabularies, the two revolutions were fundamentally different. The Americans revolted against a regime that was seen as foreign. The American War of Independence soon became an international conflict. Class distinction played little obvious part in it or in the subsequent constitutional arrangements. America's revolution owed much to England's Glorious and Bloodless Revolution of 1688–1689: both were founded in compromise and the rule of law, and culminated in moderate, representative government.

The First Modern Revolution

In contrast, until 1792 the French Revolution was essentially a civil upheaval. It was the first modern revolution. Compromise and moderation were the first victims in a bitter struggle within a splintered nation. The old order was overthrown by the sheer force of a mass movement. Violence was glorified. Echoes of the French Revolution, studied with bias and imperfectly understood, echoed through most of the popular

Popular revolt, French-style: barricades across a Moscow street during the Russian Revolution of 1905.

revolutionary movements of the 19th and 20th centuries. The Russian revolutionary Peter Kropotkin, writing in 1909, believed:

> *What we learn from the study of the Great [French] Revolution is that it was the source of all the present communist, anarchist, and socialist conceptions.*

Edmund Burke (1729–1797), whose anxiety at the swift, haphazard, and increasingly violent events taking place across the Channel prompted him to write *Reflections on the Revolution in France.*

Ironically, hostile reactions to the Revolution proved as important as the Revolution itself. They forced conservative thinkers, such as the Irish statesman Edmund Burke (*Reflections on the Revolution in France*, 1790), to put their objections to what was happening on a sound philosophical footing. Thus modern conservative thinking was born. It is also suggested that the Revolution so tarnished the name of reform that its cause was set back decades.

Forced to Be Free

The behavior of the Committee of Public Safety, and even Napoleon himself, suggested to some radicals that popular revolution *per se* was not enough. The masses, in Rousseau's words, needed to be forced to be free. Consequently, the overthrow of the old regime needed to be followed by a period of rule as harsh and inflexible as what it had replaced.

Such speculation has allowed commentators to trace a direct link between the French Revolution and Karl Marx's idea of the "dictatorship of the proletariat." This was the philosophical underpinning of the 20th-century absolutism of Lenin, Stalin, Mao, and others. With this in mind, on the bicentennial of the fall of the Bastille, Leon Daudet wrote that celebrating the French Revolution was as idiotic as celebrating the day one caught scarlet fever.

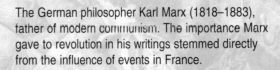

The German philosopher Karl Marx (1818–1883), father of modern communism. The importance Marx gave to revolution in his writings stemmed directly from the influence of events in France.

71

The Positive Legacy

For reasons suggested on the previous page, the French Revolution was viewed with some suspicion in the post-Marxist world that emerged at the end of the 20th century. However, links between the Revolution and later tyrannies established in the name of the people are at best arguable. We may justifiably hold the men and women of 1789–1795 responsible for their own errors and shortcomings, but not for those of the generations that followed. Moreover, if we do so, we can blind ourselves to the Revolution's more positive legacy.

The French Revolution changed forever the way people thought about politics and society. At the most basic level, it established the principle that the people are sovereign. After 1789, privilege and heredity alone could never be regarded as sufficient justification for power. The Revolution's most enduring symbol was the fall of the Bastille—people power in action. Parallels with the fall almost exactly 200 years later of another landmark of tyranny, the Berlin Wall, are not too dissimilar. Not only are the people (a term gradually expanded to embrace both genders and all races, creeds, and ages) sovereign, but they also have inalienable rights. Among these are liberty and equality, the source of true representative democracy. Interestingly, too, our vocabulary for political opinion—left and right—goes back to the habit of the radicals in the Constituent sitting to the left of the chair while their opponents sat to the right.

The Revolution, so full of optimism at the outset, ended in tragedy. But despite its failure, it left a legacy of hope: One day, somehow, its noble principles might become the foundation of a better world.

A contemporary symbol of the lasting influence of the French Revolution: the fall of the Berlin Wall, 1989. The act symbolized the triumph of the people over an unpopular regime—and offered many parallels with the fall of the Bastille exactly 200 years before.

GLOSSARY

amnesty general pardon

Ancien Régime arrangement of government and society, based on an hereditary monarchy and aristocracy, prevailing in France and most of Europe before the French Revolution

aristocracy hereditary, titled upper class

assignats bonds, supposedly backed by confiscated land, sold by the French government to raise money

bourgeoisie wealthy middle class

bureaucrat civil servant

cahiers de doléances documents presented to the Estates General that listed popular grievances and anticipated reforms

château French castle or stately home

Civil Code reformed and rationalized code of civil law produced under Napoleon's direction in 1804. Later known as the *Code Napoléon*

coalition formal association of states or parties with a common interest

commune elected local government organization set up during the Revolution and still operating today. The best known was the Commune of Paris, subdivided into sections.

Concordat formal agreement between the Pope and a civil government. Napoleon's Concordat with Pius VII (1801) remained the basis of Church–State relations in France for the rest of the 19th century.

conscription compulsory enlistment in the armed forces, usually the army

Constituent abbreviated name of the Constituent Assembly set up in 1789

constitutional monarchy monarchy in which the king or queen's role is defined by the constitution

consul one of three republican heads of state set up by the constitution of 1799. Napoleon, as First Consul, was preeminent.

Continental System ban on European trade with Britain, established by Napoleon in 1804–1805

coup forcible seizure of power by a small, well-organized group.

département one of the new administrative regions of France established in 1789

Directory five-man executive committee that dominated French government 1795–1799

émigrés people who fled from France at the time of the Revolution

Enlightenment 18th-century intellectual movement that believed that reason should be the guide in all matters

Estates General ancient assembly representing the three Estates of the French realm: the clergy, the nobles, and the commoners

executive arm of government responsible for carrying out laws and policy

exile to ban a person from his or her native land

feudalism medieval system in which landowners allowed others to use their land in exchange for service

Feuillants moderate majority of the original Jacobin Club

franchise right to vote

fraternity community spirit

grapeshot small pieces of shot fired from a cannon to cause maximum injury to enemy footsoldiers

guerrilla irregular soldier who fights with ambush and hit-and-run tactics

guild organization of craftworkers of the same industry

guillotine beheading machine developed by Dr. Joseph Guillotin as a more humane form of execution

Hébertists extreme Parisian radicals

hereditary inherited

Holy Roman Empire area of medieval Europe nominally ruled by a Holy Roman Emperor

Hôtel des Invalides military hospital in Paris that came to be used as a garrison

Jacobin belonging to the revolutionary Jacobin Club that, by 1793, had become a hotbed of radicalism

laissez-faire policy that proposes minimum government interference in economic affairs

Legislative abbreviated name for the Legislative Assembly set up in 1791

legislature law-making arm of government

Levée en Masse conscription introduced in 1793

liberalism political philosophy based on individual freedom

lycée French high school for the academically gifted

Marseillaise, La revolutionary song that became the French national anthem in 1795

Maximum price-fixing laws of 1793

militia irregular forces of ordinary citizens called up to deal with specific incidents, such as serious disorder

Mountain radical group in the Convention that instituted the Terror

nationalize remove from private ownership and put in the hands of the state

notable someone from the upper ranks of French society, a noble or bourgeois

parlement assembly of lawyers in the Ancien Régime

Patriot pro-war party led by Jacques Brissot

philosophe leading intellectual of the Enlightenment

plebiscite popular nationwide vote on a single issue, usually asking for a yes or no answer

reactionary vehemently opposed to change

representative government indirect democratic government by the people's elected representatives

republic government without a monarchy

revisionists those who organized the coup of November 1799

sansculottes Parisian radicals from the lower-middle and working classes, identified because they did not wear breeches, or culottes.

self-determination right of a nation to choose its own system of government

sovereignty ultimate political authority

stamp tax tax on documents and newspapers that had to bear a government stamp to show that the tax had been paid

suffrage right to vote in elections

Terror period of centralized government, 1793–1794, exemplified by rigorous elimination of all opposition, real and imaginary

Thermidorians those who organized the coup of July 1794 that ended the Terror

Third Estate the ordinary people of France, the non-clerical and non-noble commoners

tithe tax paid to the Church, originally consisting of one-tenth of all produce

White Terror violent attacks by reactionaries on those associated with the Revolution, including radicals and Protestants

TIMELINE OF EVENTS

1774		Accession of Louis XVI
1778–1783		France fights in American War of Independence
1787		Assembly of Notables meets
1788		Bad harvest; Estates General summoned
1789	May	Estates General meets
	June	National Assembly proclaimed
	July	Great Fear; Fall of the Bastille
	Aug.	Declaration of the Rights of Man and of the Citizen
	Aug. (onward)	*Ancien Régime* dismantled
1790	July	Civil Constitution of the Clergy
1791	June	Royal family's flight to Varennes
	Aug.	Slave rebellion in Saint-Domingue
	Oct.	Legislative Assembly meets
1792	Apr.	War with Austria
	Aug.	Monarchy overthrown
	Sept.	Convention meets
1793	Jan.	Execution of Louis XVI
	Mar.	Vendée Rebellion starts
	May	Maximum decreed
	June	Purge of Girondins from Convention
	Aug.	*Levée en Masse*
	Sept.	Terror begins

1794	July	Fall of Robespierre
1795	Oct.	Directory set up
1796		Napoleon's invasion of Italy
1799		Directory overthrown; Napoleon First Consul
1801		Concordat with Pius VII
1802		Legion of Honor established
1804		Civil Code; Napoleon becomes Emperor of the French
1805		France and Spain defeated at Battle of Trafalgar
1807		Treaty of Tilsit between France, Prussia, and Russia
1812		Napoleon's disastrous invasion of Russia
1813		France defeated at Battle of Leipzig
1814		Restoration of Louis XVIII; Napoleon exiled to Elba
1815		Napoleon returns to France; Napoleon defeated at Battle of Waterloo; Second Restoration of Louis XVIII; Napoleon exiled to St Helena

BOOKS TO READ

Of the hundreds of books about the French Revolution, the following are among the best starting points:

Dickens, Charles. *A Tale of Two Cities*. New York: New American Library, 1996.

Doyle, William. *The Oxford History of the French Revolution*. Oxford: Oxford University Press, 1990.

Forrest, Alan. *The French Revolution*. Oxford: Blackwell, 1995.

Hardman, John. *The French Revolution Sourcebook*. London: Arnold, 1999.

Hardman, John. *Robespierre*. London: Longman, 1999.

Roberts, J. M. *The French Revolution*. Oxford: Oxford University Press, 1997.

Schama, Simon. *Citizens*. New York: Viking, 1989.

Todd, Allen. *Revolutions, 1789–1917*. Cambridge: Cambridge University Press, 1998.

Townson, Duncan. *France in Revolution*. London: Hodder and Stoughton, 1990.

INDEX